The
Reference Shelf ®

Representative American Speeches 2015-2016

The Reference Shelf
Volume 88 • Number 6
H.W. Wilson
A Division of EBSCO Information Services

Published by
GREY HOUSE PUBLISHING
Amenia, New York
2016

The Reference Shelf

The books in this series contain reprints of articles, excerpts from books, addresses on current issues, and studies of social trends in the United States and other countries. There are six separately bound numbers in each volume, all of which are usually published in the same calendar year. Numbers one through five are each devoted to a single subject, providing background information and discussion from various points of view and concluding with an index and comprehensive bibliography that lists books, pamphlets, and articles on the subject. The final number of each volume is a collection of recent speeches. Books in the series may be purchased individually or on subscription.

Publisher's Cataloging-In-Publication Data
(Prepared by The Donohue Group, Inc.)

Names: H.W. Wilson Company.
Title: Representative American speeches, 2015-2016 / [compiled by] H. W. Wilson, a division of EBSCO Information Services.
Other Titles: Reference shelf ; v. 88, no. 6.
Description: Amenia, New York : Grey House Publishing, 2016. | Includes index.
Identifiers: ISBN 978-1-68217-068-7 (v.88, no.6) | ISBN 978-1-68217-062-5 (volume set)
Subjects: LCSH: Speeches, addresses, etc., American--21st century. | United States--Politics and government--2009---Sources. | Civil rights--United States--Sources. | Criminal justice, Administration of--United States--Sources. | Political campaigns--United States--History--21st century--Sources.
Classification: LCC PS661 .R46 2016 | DDC 815/.008--dc23

Contents

1

To the Graduating Class

2

Campaign Speeches

3

Civil Rights and Social Justice

4

The Year in Review

5

A Global Perspective

Preface

The best speeches—those that eloquently capture the essence of an important moment in history, give voice to an essential idea, or perfectly encapsulate the collective sentiment surrounding a profound event or ideal—can live on in history. Like Patrick Henry's "Liberty or Death" speech on the founding of the United States, or Martin Luther King Jr.'s "I Have a Dream," address at the March on Washington that became emblematic for the Civil Rights Movement, great speeches can become symbolic for the underlying events that give rise to them. In this way, important speeches form a significant part of a nation's cultural legacy and often symbolize the cultural and social impact of central figures, whether politicians, activists, entertainers, or entrepreneurs, that rise to prominence within each era. In the arenas of political discourse and social activism, speeches are often crafted to evoke an emotional response and encourage listeners to take action on key issues. Impassioned speeches populate the battleground around national and international debates, as key figures compete to sway public opinion to their side and deliver speeches that may potentially one day be seen as pivotal moments in larger social movements.

In the digital age, the nature of public speaking has changed. Each year, the passionate speeches given by politicians, social activists, broadcasters, and other public figures become part of a vast sea of information competing for attention. Thanks to digital media and connectivity, a speech given at a regional bookstore in suburban Iowa has the potential to become national or even international news, but, on the other side of the coin, important, essential addresses by some of an era's greatest thinkers and speakers can easily be lost when competing with sensational ideas and opinions. In addition, the fact that any speech or public address might now be subject to global consumption means that those who choose to speak publically must accept the challenge of framing their remarks for broader audiences, considering the impact that their words might have on people or groups for whom the speech was never originally intended. The popularity of the TED Talks series, which runs under the slogan "Ideas Worth Spreading" and invites a vast array of speakers from marketing professionals to social activists to speak in digital presentations, has attracted international attention and millions of viewers, demonstrating that public oration still has considerable popular appeal. The essential speeches of 2016 were marked by passionate dissonance and emotional poignancy as politicians, activists, celebrities, and other public figures reflected on the many difficult challenges facing an increasingly globalized world, and on the tragedies, contentious cultural debates, and heartening victories that helped to define the year and, by extension, the entire era.

Speaking to the Future: Commencement Speeches and the Political Campaign

Certain kinds of speeches are focused on the future, exploring how human life or society might or should change or espousing hopes for future generations and eras of human existence. Such speeches are typically delivered to accompany transformative events, such as the speeches that accompany school graduation or commencement ceremonies. Similarly, campaign speeches mark a political era and so often involve reflection on the past and present state of the nation, the state, or the world (whether negative or positive) with inspiring messages of hope that encourage listeners (and more often readers) to imagine a renewed political era that could lead to a more prosperous future.

Colleges and universities have long served as an important forum for public speaking. Commencement speeches, in general, give speakers an opportunity to speak about the value and values of education and to reflect on the role of education in the public and global spheres. The commencement and graduation speeches of 2016 covered a variety of issues, including the human future of work in the Digital Age, the importance of critical thinking and the scientific approach to innovation and problem solving, and the effect of educational institutions on American prosperity. One of the most interesting themes in the year's educational speeches was the discussion of how today's students must balance personal achievement with social responsibility, a theme that reflected some of the year's most pressing global debates.

Political speeches occupy a unique place in the field of public speaking, being both calls for political mobilization and marketing messages designed to attract voters to a political product, which may be as narrowly conceived as a single referendum or candidacy or as broad as an entire political worldview. In a campaign season widely derided due to contentious campaigns that relied heavily on mudslinging and personal attacks, 2016's politicians struggled to craft speeches that could reach out to a seemingly cynical electorate. On the Democrats' side, the passionate public response to the populist message of Bernie Sanders revealed a growing divide between progressive and more moderate liberals, while the unexpected popularity of Donald Trump's inflammatory campaign saw the Republican Party fractured and unable to gather support for their mainstream candidates. As a result, speakers on both sides called for their parties to unify behind their chosen candidates, while others eschewed conciliatory messages in favor of accusatory rhetoric, thereby deepening the dissatisfaction among the electorate.

During the campaign, Mr. Trump and supporters revived a perennial, if suspect, assertion that corporate leadership is substantively similar to national leadership, and therefore that Trump's experience as an entrepreneur qualified him to lead a nation. Trump's speeches, and those of his supporters, were light on specific policy recommendations but appealed to the most optimistic hopes of those who feel disenfranchised within US society and blame current Democratic leaders for theirs and the nation's problems. On key, highly complex issues that the nation's leading political, social, and educational leaders have struggled with for years—such as domestic and foreign terrorism, the state of US education, the threat of crime, and the lamentable state of the working-class economy—Trump encouraged voters to believe that politicians (especially Clinton and other Democratic leaders) have been ignorant of seemingly simple, though unexplained, strategies that will enable Trump to solve the nation's key issues, as he repeatedly asserted, "very, very, quickly." Trump's supporters, including House Speaker Paul Ryan, and a host of entrepreneurs, denounced Democratic leadership and argued that a radical departure from the political establishment was needed to fix the nation.

Clinton and her supporters, by contrast, were faced with a far different challenge. Clinton entered the race with low approval ratings based on a panoply of complaints including aesthetic criticisms about the sound of her voice and "cold" demeanor, broad ideological accusations that framed her as a member of a political elite out of touch with average Americans, and specific criticisms regarding her positions on key policy issues and complicity in encouraging the US military's aggressive foreign policy during the ongoing War on Terror. Clinton, Barack Obama, Michelle Obama, and numerous other party members gave speeches that highlighted the successes of the Obama administration (for which Clinton played an important role) and used Clinton's experience and four decades of public service to argue that she was the more qualified candidate. The broader cultural importance of Clinton's campaign—being the first woman to be nominated by a major political party, was an underlying theme of the election and one that some speakers used as a segue to speak about the continued challenges faced by women striving for social, political, and economic equality. However, the significance of the campaign as a pivotal point in women's history was largely overshadowed by the widespread antiestablishment messages on both sides of the campaign.

Speaking to the Moment: Political Activism, Social Justice, and the Annual Review

While some speeches are aimed at motivating listeners or readers to prepare for a coming change and a new future, others are focused less on a specific goal and more on encouraging generalized interest or action around a current issue. Among speeches in this broad category are those that accompany annual events, like the Academy Awards or the Superbowl, at which athletes and other celebrities with an interest in activism can use the national platform to speak out about important issues. Similarly, each year there are numerous speeches that summarize the events of the past year and help to frame the progress, or lack thereof, towards national and international goals.

The passionate and ongoing debate surrounding racial injustice continued in 2016. The Black Lives Matter movement began in 2013 following the widely publicized trial of George Zimmerman, who was acquitted of murdering African-American teen Trayvon Martin. Black Lives Matter garnered national attention in 2014 following the police killing of Michael Brown in Ferguson, Missouri and Eric Garner in New York City. As the movement spread through social media, inspiring protests and demonstrations around the world, it became a centerpiece for one of the most intense debates on racial injustice since the Civil Rights era.

Many have misunderstood the symbolic name and further the essential meaning of the movement, believing erroneously that the "Black Lives Matter" slogan is meant to assert that African-American lives are more important than other lives.

Operating under this misconception, some have attempted to counter the Black Lives Matter movement by asserting that "All Lives Matter" or with the counter-movement "Blue Lives Matter," in support of police. The correct meaning of "Black Lives Matter" is to call attention to the fact that African-American lives are and have been *undervalued* in American society and that changes are needed to achieve a state in which African-American lives are afforded the *same* value as white lives or the "blue" lives of police officers.

In 2016, numerous politicians, celebrities, and activists mentioned the Black Lives Matter movement and commented on racism among police and in the US justice system. A number of high profile African-American celebrities and athletes, for instance, used the year's awards celebrations and high-profile entertainment events as platforms to speak out on racial equality. President Obama, in a speech at the debut of the National Museum of African American History and Culture, also touched on the Black Lives Matter movement, and expressed his hope that a more nuanced recognition of the path that African-American people have traveled from slavery to the present can help stimulate progressive dialogues on race and a broader recognition of the work still needed to achieve racial equality.

Another social issue that garnered significant press during 2015 and 2016 was the debate over transgender bathroom access, with some believing that transgendered individuals should use bathrooms according to their sex at birth, while others arguing that all individuals should be allowed to use bathrooms that align with their gender identity or that all public restrooms should be gender neutral. The debate over the issue was misinformed by broadly inflammatory claims that permitting individuals to use bathrooms aligning with gender identity would open the door to rape and sexual misconduct. The year saw one of the most intense battles over bathroom rights in North Carolina, where the state passed a law requiring individuals to use bathrooms in keeping with their gender at birth. The issue is especially important in schools, where individuals have no choice but to use public bathroom facilities and so laws restricting individuals from using bathrooms aligning with their gender identity could be psychologically damaging to children at various ages. The restroom rights debate is also part of a larger struggle for LGBT equality and acceptance in the United States, which is an issue that was brought into sharp focus by the tragic June 12th attack on Orlando's Pulse nightclub. While some framed the Orlando tragedy as a terrorist event, given that the attacker claimed to have been inspired by Islamic extremism, it was also a hate crime and one that served to motivate meaningful, emotional speeches on the value of tolerance and solidarity.

Speaking to the World

The year's activists, politicians, and celebrities reflected on the state of the nation, but also on the state of the world. Many speeches of 2016 focused on globalization and the interconnectedness of the world's relationships. Events in Europe like the refugee crisis on the continent's southern border and the controversial vote by the United Kingdom to leave the European Union were major events that set the stage for numerous debates and speeches, both in favor of and dramatically opposed to international trade agreements, foreign aid, immigration, and a variety of other facets of the larger phenomenon. This debate, which is also reflected in the controversial Trans-Pacific Partnership, echoes an age-old disagreement over the benefits of isolationism versus globalism, and the degree to which nations should take part in a global community or should place the needs of their own ahead of international concerns.

Pressing global issues, like the ongoing Syrian refugee crisis, have infused the globalization debate with renewed significance and poignancy, while, behind the international media's focus on global economics, globalization also touches on humanity's foremost truly planetary concern, human-caused climate change and the degradation of natural resources. Environmental management has been a key issue every year since the beginning of the climate change debate and 2016 saw a number of passionate speeches calling for more intense public pressure on political leaders to create policies that will be more effective at protecting the world's oceans and other threatened habitats. While the US presidential election and other sociological debates in many ways eclipsed environmentalist concerns in 2016, the environmental debate is far from trivial, with an overwhelming majority of experts and scientists in agreement that climate change is among the greatest threats to humankind in the history of the species.

Micah L. Issitt

1
To the Graduating Class

Al Drago/CQ Roll

President Barack Obama speaks during the 148th commencement ceremony at Howard University May 7, 2016 in Washington, DC.

Address by Vice President Joseph Biden on Receiving the 2016 Laetare Medal at the University of Notre Dame

By Joe Biden

In receiving the Laetare Medal at the University of Notre Dame, Vice President Joe Biden reflects on his long friendship with John Boehner and their twenty-five-year working relationship, finding political common ground as members of opposing political parties. The Laetare Medal is given by the university in recognition of outstanding service to the Catholic Church and society. Former Speaker of the House John Boehner jointly received the medal with Biden, the oldest and most prestigious award accorded to American Catholics. "We live in a toxic political environment where poisonous invective and partisan gamesmanship pass for political leadership," said Rev. John I. Jenkins, C.S.C., Notre Dame's president. "Public confidence in government is at historic lows, and cynicism is high. It is a good time to remind ourselves what lives dedicated to genuine public service in politics look like." Joe Biden Jr. is the 47th and current vice president of the United States. Biden served as a United States senator representing Delaware from 1973 to 2009.

Let's get something straight right off the bat. I don't like John Boehner. I love him. Father Jenkins, Notre Dame, thank you. Thank you for this honor—the Laetare Medal. I can say, without fear of contradiction, it is the most meaningful award I've ever received in my life. And my mother Catherine Eugenia Finnegan, I wish she were here, but she's looking down to see me receive this.

But I must say, Father Jenkins, my grandfather, Ambrose Finnegan, who played for Santa Clara at the turn of the century and was a newspaperman at Scranton, always resented Notre Dame. Because Santa Clara had a football team, particularly in the teens and '20s and '30s, referred to as the Notre Dame of the West. He said, "Hell, they're the Santa Clara of the Midwest." Grandpop, forgive me. I played football at the University of Delaware and in high school, and I finally made it to the 50-yard line in Notre Dame Stadium, man. This is worth the trip, man. You all think I'm kidding. I'm not.

Father, you said that politics is a full-contact sport. I agree. But Father, to the detriment of the nation in my view, and I think John would agree with me, it has recently become a blood sport full of invective and ad hominem arguments. I've been there a long time. John and I served together for over 25 years. I've been elected to

Delivered on May 15, 2016, at the University of Notre Dame in South Bend, Indiana by Vice President Joseph Biden.

the Senate seven times and vice president twice. I've not seen it like this in my career. You quoted the Holy Father, Father, when you said he addressed the joint session of Congress, he said, our responsibility was to the tireless demanding pursuit of the common good, the chief aim of politics.

Father, I've had the privilege of spending time, as John did, with the Holy Father. He not only consoled me and my family when I lost my Beau, but when I met him representing the United States at his inauguration, and I walked up with other heads of state to be formally introduced to him in the Basilica, a monsignor who I had just spent time with earlier because I had been meeting with Pope Benedict—I hope I wasn't the reason he resigned—turned to introduce me to the Holy Father. And before he could, the Holy Father put out his hand and said, "Mr. Vice President, you are always welcome here. You are always welcome here." Think about him. That's the message he has sent to the world. It's the reason why he is the most respected man in the world as I speak here today. Not just among Catholics, but Muslims, Hindus, other Christians, the Jewish community. That's not hyperbole, he literally is the most respected man in the world. You are always welcome here. And I believe the message he was urging the Congress was to extend to everyone, we who hold high public office, to extend our hand as Americans and say, "You are always welcome here."

I was raised by parents who are the embodiment of Catholic social doctrine. I was taught by the Sisters of Saint Joseph and the Norbertine priests in high school, "everyone is always welcome in my home." I was taught by my mother that no one was better than me but that everyone was my equal.

I was taught by my father—who struggled—that every man, every woman, he meant everyone regardless of their station of life, regardless of whether or not you agreed with them, was entitled to be treated with dignity and respect. My father used to say that the greatest sin of all was the abuse of power whether economic, political, psychological or physical. He's the reason that I wrote the Violence Against Women legislation. He abhorred the notion of the abuse of power, totally consistent with what his Holiness talks about now and what our Roman Catholic faith has taught us for over 2,000 years.

I was taught by my family and my faith that a good life at its core—and this is why I truly like John—is about being personal. It all gets down to being personal. Being engaged. I was taught by my family and my faith to look beyond the caricature of a person and to resist the temptation when you disagree to ascribe a negative motive, because when you do that, number one, you don't truly know what that person's motive is, and number two, it makes it virtually impossible to reach common ground. I was taught by my family and my faith never to confuse academic credentials and social sophistication with gravitas and judgment. To have the heart to strive to distinguish between what is meaningful and what is ephemeral, the head to know the difference between knowledge and judgment.

But most importantly, my family and our faith warned me against the temptation of rationalizing in the pursuit of ambition. "I know it's her birthday, but she won't mind, this is an important business trip." "I know it's his last game, but I'd have to take the red-eye back to see it, he'll understand." "I know we've been planning this family vacation for a long, long time, but I have such an opportunity if I leave." It's not only wrong, but if you engage in this rationalization, which everyone does, never underestimate the ability of the human mind to rationalize.

But If you do, it will become very difficult to weather the storm when reality intrudes. And it will. Reality will intrude. In 1972 I was elected the second youngest man in the history of the United States of America. I was 29 years old; I wasn't old enough to be sworn in. I had to wait 13 days to be eligible. Forty-one days later, reality intruded. I was in Washington hiring my staff when I got a phone call. A tractor-trailer had broadsided my wife and my three children. Killed my wife and killed my daughter. And for my two boys—it was uncertain—who, thank God, later fully recovered. Being elected at 29 to the Senate is pretty heady stuff. It's the stuff of which ambition can get out of hand. Reality intruded. Forty-two years later, it happened again. Many of your parents and people in the audience have gone through worse than I have. They know. Many of you know.

My soul, my son, my Beau, the attorney general in the state of Delaware, the most respected political figure in the state, having volunteered as a U.S. attorney to go to Kosovo to help them set up a criminal justice system during the war. And John, I just learned that the president of Kosovo is naming a street after my son, the Major Joseph R. Biden Boulevard. He then volunteered as attorney general—he had to get an exception, because you become federal property when you're in the National Guard—to go to Iraq for a year.

A year later, he came home a decorated soldier, awarded the Bronze Star, the Legion of Merit, the Delaware Conspicuous Service Cross, the best physical shape of his life. While running 10 miles, had to lay down. He was diagnosed with stage 4 glioblastoma in the brain. Two years later it took him, after a heroic struggle.

John talked about, my father talked about, you just gotta get up. My son's last words to me were, "Dad, I'm not afraid. Promise me you'll be all right." My dad had an expression. He'd say: "Never complain and never explain." Beau never, ever did. And I think back on it. What would happen if John and I only followed our ambition? Thank God I never missed Neilia's birthday, or an important thing. Thank God I never missed his game for an unimportant political event. I think Beau said it best, and I say it to all of you, when he was attorney general during a commencement speech he was giving—he went to Penn and he went to Syracuse Law School in 2011. Here's what he said. He said, "You'll find peace when there are certain rules that are not malleable. Your conscience, your conscience should not be malleable. Your values for another. These are the means along with the learning you now possess. They are the things that will guide you. They'll also be the things to save you."

Father, I've read some accounts how John and I are "old school." We used to treat each other with respect, hang out with each other. John and I aren't old school, we're the American school. We're what you have to restore. Where progress only comes when you deal with your opponent with respect, listening as well as talking.

Class of 2016, this is not hyperbole, you're the best educated, most tolerant generation in the history of the United States of America. So engage. Engage in the tireless pursuit of finding common ground because not only will you be happier, you will be incredibly more successful. That's where you'll find your reward and it'll make us all better for it. It's a true honor to be here with John. It's a great honor to receive this medal. May God bless you all. And may God protect our troops.

Print Citations

CMS: Biden, Joe. "Address by Vice President Joseph Biden on Receiving the 2016 Laetare Medal at the University of Notre Dame." Speech presented at the University of Notre Dame, South Bend, IN, May, 2016. In *The Reference Shelf: Representative American Speeches 2015-2016*, edited by Betsy Maury, 3-6. Ipswich, MA: H.W. Wilson, 2016.

MLA: Biden, Joe. "Address by Vice President Joseph Biden on Receiving the 2016 Laetare Medal at the University of Notre Dame." University of Notre Dame. South Bend, IN. May, 2016. Presentation. *The Reference Shelf: Representative American Speeches 2015-2016*. Ed. Betsy Maury. Ipswich: H.W. Wilson, 2016. 3-6. Print.

APA: Biden, J. (2016). Address by vice president Joseph Biden on receiving the 2016 Laetare medal at the University of Notre Dame. [Presentation]. *Speech presented at the University of Notre Dame*. South Bend, IN. In Betsy Maury (Ed.), *The reference shelf: Representative American speeches 2015-2016* (pp. 3-5). Ipswich, MA: H.W. Wilson. (Original work published 2016)

Commencement Address to the Howard University Class of 2016

By Barack Obama

President Barack Obama in his last term as US President reflects on the history and mission of Howard University and toasts its graduates past and present. The university that was borne out of the Freedman's Bureau was established shortly after the Emancipation Proclamation, and embodies the upward mobility dream of many black Americans. President Obama talks about the importance of understanding the history and struggles of those who came before to create opportunities for this generation to succeed. He emphasizes that black Americans must recognize the work that has been done in improving poverty and race relations in America thus far. He firmly tells graduates to be mindful of progress and that 2016 is a far better year to graduate than any other year before. The president urges graduates to use their passion and unique abilities to take action with a deliberate strategy in making continued progress in changing the world. President Barack Obama is the 44th president of the United States, having been elected to office in 2008 and reelected in 2012. Prior to becoming president, Obama was a United States senator representing the state of Illinois from 2005 to 2008.

THE PRESIDENT: Thank you! Hello, Howard! (Applause.) H-U!

AUDIENCE: You know!

THE PRESIDENT: H-U!

AUDIENCE: You know!

THE PRESIDENT: (Laughter.) Thank you so much, everybody. Please, please, have a seat. Oh, I feel important now. Got a degree from Howard. Cicely Tyson said something nice about me. (Laughter.)

AUDIENCE MEMBER: I love you, President!

THE PRESIDENT: I love you back.

To President Frederick, the Board of Trustees, faculty and staff, fellow recipients of honorary degrees, thank you for the honor of spending this day with you. And congratulations to the Class of 2016! (Applause.) Four years ago, back when you were just freshmen, I understand many of you came by my house the night I was reelected. (Laughter.) So I decided to return the favor and come by yours.

To the parents, the grandparents, aunts, uncles, brothers, sisters, all the family and friends who stood by this class, cheered them on, helped them get here

---

Delivered on May 17, 2016, at Howard University in Washington, DC by President Barack Obama.

today—this is your day, as well. Let's give them a big round of applause, as well. (Applause.)

I'm not trying to stir up any rivalries here; I just want to see who's in the house. We got Quad? (Applause.) Annex. (Applause.) Drew. Carver. Slow. Towers. And Meridian. (Applause.) Rest in peace, Meridian. (Laughter.) Rest in peace.

I know you're all excited today. You might be a little tired, as well. Some of you were up all night making sure your credits were in order. (Laughter.) Some of you stayed up too late, ended up at HoChi at 2:00 a.m. (Laughter.) Got some mambo sauce on your fingers. (Laughter.)

But you got here. And you've all worked hard to reach this day. You've shuttled between challenging classes and Greek life. You've led clubs, played an instrument or a sport. You volunteered, you interned. You held down one, two, maybe three jobs. You've made lifelong friends and discovered exactly what you're made of. The "Howard Hustle" has strengthened your sense of purpose and ambition.

Which means you're part of a long line of Howard graduates. Some are on this stage today. Some are in the audience. That spirit of achievement and special responsibility has defined this campus ever since the Freedman's Bureau established Howard just four years after the Emancipation Proclamation; just two years after the Civil War came to an end. They created this university with a vision—a vision of uplift; a vision for an America where our fates would be determined not by our race, gender, religion or creed, but where we would be free—in every sense—to pursue our individual and collective dreams.

It is that spirit that's made Howard a centerpiece of African-American intellectual life and a central part of our larger American story. This institution has been the home of many firsts: The first black Nobel Peace Prize winner. The first black Supreme Court justice. But its mission has been to ensure those firsts were not the last. Countless scholars, professionals, artists, and leaders from every field received their training here. The generations of men and women who walked through this yard helped reform our government, cure disease, grow a black middle class, advance civil rights, shape our culture. The seeds of change—for all Americans—were sown here. And that's what I want to talk about today.

As I was preparing these remarks, I realized that when I was first elected President, most of you—the Class of 2016—were just starting high school. Today, you're graduating college. I used to joke about being old. Now I realize I'm old. (Laughter.) It's not a joke anymore. (Laughter.)

But seeing all of you here gives me some perspective. It makes me reflect on the changes that I've seen over my own lifetime. So let me begin with what may sound like a controversial statement—a hot take.

Given the current state of our political rhetoric and debate, let me say something that may be controversial, and that is this: America is a better place today than it was when I graduated from college. (Applause.) Let me repeat: America is by almost every measure better than it was when I graduated from college. It also happens to be better off than when I took office—(laughter)—but that's a longer story. (Applause.) That's a different discussion for another speech.

But think about it. I graduated in 1983. New York City, America's largest city, where I lived at the time, had endured a decade marked by crime and deterioration and near bankruptcy. And many cities were in similar shape. Our nation had gone through years of economic stagnation, the stranglehold of foreign oil, a recession where unemployment nearly scraped 11 percent. The auto industry was getting its clock cleaned by foreign competition. And don't even get me started on the clothes and the hairstyles. I've tried to eliminate all photos of me from this period. I thought I looked good. (Laughter.) I was wrong.

Since that year—since the year I graduated—the poverty rate is down. Americans with college degrees, that rate is up. Crime rates are down. America's cities have undergone a renaissance. There are more women in the workforce. They're earning more money. We've cut teen pregnancy in half. We've slashed the African American dropout rate by almost 60 percent, and all of you have a computer in your pocket that gives you the world at the touch of a button. In 1983, I was part of fewer than 10 percent of African Americans who graduated with a bachelor's degree. Today, you're part of the more than 20 percent who will. And more than half of blacks say we're better off than our parents were at our age—and that our kids will be better off, too.

So America is better. And the world is better, too. A wall came down in Berlin. An Iron Curtain was torn asunder. The obscenity of apartheid came to an end. A young generation in Belfast and London have grown up without ever having to think about IRA bombings. In just the past 16 years, we've come from a world without marriage equality to one where it's a reality in nearly two dozen countries. Around the world, more people live in democracies. We've lifted more than 1 billion people from extreme poverty. We've cut the child mortality rate worldwide by more than half.

America is better. The world is better. And stay with me now—race relations are better since I graduated. That's the truth. No, my election did not create a post-racial society. I don't know who was propagating that notion. That was not mine. But the election itself—and the subsequent one—because the first one, folks might have made a mistake. (Laughter.) The second one, they knew what they were getting. The election itself was just one indicator of how attitudes had changed.

In my inaugural address, I remarked that just 60 years earlier, my father might not have been served in a D.C. restaurant—at least not certain of them. There were no black CEOs of Fortune 500 companies. Very few black judges. Shoot, as Larry Wilmore pointed out last week, a lot of folks didn't even think blacks had the tools to be a quarterback. Today, former Bull Michael Jordan isn't just the greatest basketball player of all time—he owns the team. (Laughter.) When I was graduating, the main black hero on TV was Mr. T. (Laughter.) Rap and hip hop were counterculture, underground. Now, Shonda Rhimes owns Thursday night, and Beyoncé runs the world. (Laughter.) We're no longer only entertainers, we're producers, studio executives. No longer small business owners—we're CEOs, we're mayors, representatives, Presidents of the United States. (Applause.)

I am not saying gaps do not persist. Obviously, they do. Racism persists.

Inequality persists. Don't worry—I'm going to get to that. But I wanted to start, Class of 2016, by opening your eyes to the moment that you are in. If you had to choose one moment in history in which you could be born, and you didn't know ahead of time who you were going to be—what nationality, what gender, what race, whether you'd be rich or poor, gay or straight, what faith you'd be born into—you wouldn't choose 100 years ago. You wouldn't choose the fifties, or the sixties, or the seventies. You'd choose right now. If you had to choose a time to be, in the words of Lorraine Hansberry, "young, gifted, and black" in America, you would choose right now. (Applause.)

I tell you all this because it's important to note progress. Because to deny how far we've come would do a disservice to the cause of justice, to the legions of foot soldiers; to not only the incredibly accomplished individuals who have already been mentioned, but your mothers and your dads, and grandparents and great-grandparents, who marched and toiled and suffered and overcame to make this day possible. I tell you this not to lull you into complacency, but to spur you into action—because there's still so much more work to do, so many more miles to travel. And America needs you to gladly, happily take up that work. You all have some work to do. So enjoy the party, because you're going to be busy. (Laughter.)

Yes, our economy has recovered from crisis stronger than almost any other in the world. But there are folks of all races who are still hurting—who still can't find work that pays enough to keep the lights on, who still can't save for retirement. We've still got a big racial gap in economic opportunity. The overall unemployment rate is 5 percent, but the black unemployment rate is almost nine. We've still got an achievement gap when black boys and girls graduate high school and college at lower rates than white boys and white girls. Harriet Tubman may be going on the twenty, but we've still got a gender gap when a black woman working full-time still earns just 66 percent of what a white man gets paid. (Applause.)

We've got a justice gap when too many black boys and girls pass through a pipeline from underfunded schools to overcrowded jails. This is one area where things have gotten worse. When I was in college, about half a million people in America were behind bars. Today, there are about 2.2 million. Black men are about six times likelier to be in prison right now than white men.

Around the world, we've still got challenges to solve that threaten everybody in the 21st century—old scourges like disease and conflict, but also new challenges, from terrorism and climate change.

So make no mistake, Class of 2016—you've got plenty of work to do. But as complicated and sometimes intractable as these challenges may seem, the truth is that your generation is better positioned than any before you to meet those challenges, to flip the script.

Now, how you do that, how you meet these challenges, how you bring about change will ultimately be up to you. My generation, like all generations, is too confined by our own experience, too invested in our own biases, too stuck in our ways to provide much of the new thinking that will be required. But us old-heads have learned a few things that might be useful in your journey. So with the rest of my time, I'd like to offer some suggestions for how young leaders like you can fulfill your destiny and shape our collective future—bend it in the direction of justice and equality and freedom.

First of all—and this should not be a problem for this group—be confident in your heritage. (Applause.) Be confident in your blackness. One of the great changes that's occurred in our country since I was your age is the realization there's no one way to be black. Take it from somebody who's seen both sides of debate about whether I'm black enough. (Laughter.) In the past couple months, I've had lunch with the Queen of England and hosted Kendrick Lamar in the Oval Office. There's no straitjacket, there's no constraints, there's no litmus test for authenticity.

Look at Howard. One thing most folks don't know about Howard is how diverse it is. When you arrived here, some of you were like, oh, they've got black people in Iowa? (Laughter.) But it's true—this class comes from big cities and rural communities, and some of you crossed oceans to study here. You shatter stereotypes. Some of you come from a long line of Bison. Some of you are the first in your family to graduate from college. (Applause.) You all talk different, you all dress different. You're Lakers fans, Celtics fans, maybe even some hockey fans. (Laughter.)

And because of those who've come before you, you have models to follow. You can work for a company, or start your own. You can go into politics, or run an organization that holds politicians accountable. You can write a book that wins the National Book Award, or you can write the new run of "Black Panther." Or, like one of your alumni, Ta-Nehisi Coates, you can go ahead and just do both. You can create your own style, set your own standard of beauty, embrace your own sexuality. Think about an icon we just lost—Prince. He blew up categories. People didn't know what Prince was doing. (Laughter.) And folks loved him for it.

You need to have the same confidence. Or as my daughters tell me all the time, "You be you, Daddy." (Laughter.) Sometimes Sasha puts a variation on it—"You do you, Daddy." (Laughter.) And because you're a black person doing whatever it is that you're doing, that makes it a black thing. Feel confident.

Second, even as we each embrace our own beautiful, unique, and valid versions of our blackness, remember the tie that does bind us as African Americans—and that is our particular awareness of injustice and unfairness and struggle. That means we cannot sleepwalk through life. We cannot be ignorant of history. (Applause.) We can't meet the world with a sense of entitlement. We can't walk by a homeless man without asking why a society as wealthy as ours allows that state of affairs to occur. We can't just lock up a low-level dealer without asking why this boy, barely out of childhood, felt he had no other options. We have cousins and uncles and brothers and sisters who we remember were just as smart and just as talented as we were, but somehow got ground down by structures that are unfair and unjust.

And that means we have to not only question the world as it is, and stand up for those African Americans who haven't been so lucky—because, yes, you've worked hard, but you've also been lucky. That's a pet peeve of mine: People who have been successful and don't realize they've been lucky. That God may have blessed them; it wasn't nothing you did. So don't have an attitude. But we must expand our moral imaginations to understand and empathize with all people who are struggling, not just black folks who are struggling—the refugee, the immigrant, the rural poor, the transgender person, and yes, the middle-aged white guy who you may think has all the advantages, but over the last several decades has seen his world upended by economic and cultural and technological change, and feels powerless to stop it. You got to get in his head, too.

Number three: You have to go through life with more than just passion for change; you need a strategy. I'll repeat that. I want you to have passion, but you have to have a strategy. Not just awareness, but action. Not just hashtags, but votes.

You see, change requires more than righteous anger. It requires a program, and it requires organizing. At the 1964 Democratic Convention, Fannie Lou Hamer—all five-feet-four-inches tall—gave a fiery speech on the national stage. But then she went back home to Mississippi and organized cotton pickers. And she didn't have the tools and technology where you can whip up a movement in minutes. She had to go door to door. And I'm so proud of the new guard of black civil rights leaders who understand this. It's thanks in large part to the activism of young people like many of you, from Black Twitter to Black Lives Matter, that America's eyes have been opened—white, black, Democrat, Republican—to the real problems, for example, in our criminal justice system.

But to bring about structural change, lasting change, awareness is not enough. It requires changes in law, changes in custom. If you care about mass incarceration, let me ask you: How are you pressuring members of Congress to pass the criminal justice reform bill now pending before them? (Applause.) If you care about better policing, do you know who your district attorney is? Do you know who your state's attorney general is? Do you know the difference? Do you know who appoints the police chief and who writes the police training manual? Find out who they are, what their responsibilities are. Mobilize the community, present them with a plan, work with them to bring about change, hold them accountable if they do not deliver. Passion is vital, but you've got to have a strategy.

And your plan better include voting—not just some of the time, but all the time. (Applause.) It is absolutely true that 50 years after the Voting Rights Act, there are still too many barriers in this country to vote. There are too many people trying to erect new barriers to voting. This is the only advanced democracy on Earth that goes out of its way to make it difficult for people to vote. And there's a reason for that. There's a legacy to that.

But let me say this: Even if we dismantled every barrier to voting, that alone would not change the fact that America has some of the lowest voting rates in the free world. In 2014, only 36 percent of Americans turned out to vote in the midterms—the second-lowest participation rate on record. Youth turnout—that would be you—was less than 20 percent. Less than 20 percent. Four out of five did not vote. In 2012, nearly two in three African Americans turned out. And then, in 2014, only two in five turned out. You don't think that made a difference in terms of the Congress I've got to deal with? And then people are wondering, well, how come Obama hasn't gotten this done? How come he didn't get that done? You don't think that made a difference? What would have happened if you had turned out at 50, 60, 70 percent, all across this country? People try to make this political thing really complicated. Like, what kind of reforms do we need? And how do we need to do that? You know what, just vote. It's math. If you have more votes than the other guy, you get to do what you want. (Laughter.) It's not that complicated.

And you don't have excuses. You don't have to guess the number of jellybeans in a jar or bubbles on a bar of soap to register to vote. You don't have to risk your life to cast a ballot. Other people already did that for you. (Applause.) Your grand-parents, your great-grandparents might be here today if they were working on it. What's your excuse? When we don't vote, we give away our power, disenfranchise ourselves—right when we need to use the power that we have; right when we need your power to stop others from taking away the vote and rights of those more vulner-able than you are—the elderly and the poor, the formerly incarcerated trying to earn their second chance.

So you got to vote all the time, not just when it's cool, not just when it's time to elect a President, not just when you're inspired. It's your duty. When it's time to elect a member of Congress or a city councilman, or a school board member, or a sheriff. That's how we change our politics—by electing people at every level who are representative of and accountable to us. It is not that complicated. Don't make it complicated.

And finally, change requires more than just speaking out—it requires listening, as well. In particular, it requires listening to those with whom you disagree, and being prepared to compromise. When I was a state senator, I helped pass Illinois's first racial profiling law, and one of the first laws in the nation requiring the video-taping of confessions in capital cases. And we were successful because, early on, I engaged law enforcement. I didn't say to them, oh, you guys are so racist, you need to do something. I understood, as many of you do, that the overwhelming majority of police officers are good, and honest, and courageous, and fair, and love the com-munities they serve.

And we knew there were some bad apples, and that even the good cops with the best of intentions—including, by the way, African American police officers—might have unconscious biases, as we all do. So we engaged and we listened, and we kept working until we built consensus. And because we took the time to listen, we crafted legislation that was good for the police—because it improved the trust and cooperation of the community—and it was good for the communities, who were less likely to be treated unfairly. And I can say this unequivocally: Without at least the acceptance of the police organizations in Illinois, I could never have gotten those bills passed. Very simple. They would have blocked them.

The point is, you need allies in a democracy. That's just the way it is. It can be frustrating and it can be slow. But history teaches us that the alternative to democracy is always worse. That's not just true in this country. It's not a black or white thing. Go to any country where the give and take of democracy has been repealed by one-party rule, and I will show you a country that does not work.

And democracy requires compromise, even when you are 100 percent right. This is hard to explain sometimes. You can be completely right, and you still are going to have to engage folks who disagree with you. If you think that the only way forward is to be as uncompromising as possible, you will feel good about yourself, you will enjoy a certain moral purity, but you're not going to get what you want. And if you don't get what you want long enough, you will eventually think the whole system is rigged. And that will lead to more cynicism, and less participation, and a downward spiral of more injustice and more anger and more despair. And that's never been the source of our progress. That's how we cheat ourselves of progress.

We remember Dr. King's soaring oratory, the power of his letter from a Birmingham jail, the marches he led. But he also sat down with President Johnson in the Oval Office to try and get a Civil Rights Act and a Voting Rights Act passed. And those two seminal bills were not perfect—just like the Emancipation Proclamation was a war document as much as it was some clarion call for freedom. Those mileposts of our progress were not perfect. They did not make up for centuries of slavery or Jim Crow or eliminate racism or provide for 40 acres and a mule. But they made things better. And you know what, I will take better every time. I always tell my staff—better is good, because you consolidate your gains and then you move on to the next fight from a stronger position.

Brittany Packnett, a member of the Black Lives Matter movement and Campaign Zero, one of the Ferguson protest organizers, she joined our Task Force on 21st Century Policing. Some of her fellow activists questioned whether she should participate. She rolled up her sleeves and sat at the same table with big city police chiefs and prosecutors. And because she did, she ended up shaping many of the recommendations of that task force. And those recommendations are now being adopted across the country—changes that many of the protesters called for. If young activists like Brittany had refused to participate out of some sense of ideological purity, then those great ideas would have just remained ideas. But she did participate. And that's how change happens.

America is big and it is boisterous and it is more diverse than ever. The president told me that we've got a significant Nepalese contingent here at Howard. I would not have guessed that. Right on. But it just tells you how interconnected we're becoming. And with so many folks from so many places, converging, we are not always going to agree with each other.

Another Howard alum, Zora Neale Hurston, once said—this is a good quote here: "Nothing that God ever made is the same thing to more than one person." Think about that. That's why our democracy gives us a process designed for us to settle our disputes with argument and ideas and votes instead of violence and simple majority rule.

So don't try to shut folks out, don't try to shut them down, no matter how much you might disagree with them. There's been a trend around the country of trying to get colleges to disinvite speakers with a different point of view, or disrupt a politician's rally. Don't do that—no matter how ridiculous or offensive you might find the things that come out of their mouths. Because as my grandmother used to tell me, every time a fool speaks, they are just advertising their own ignorance. Let them talk. Let them talk. If you don't, you just make them a victim, and then they can avoid accountability.

That doesn't mean you shouldn't challenge them. Have the confidence to challenge them, the confidence in the rightness of your position. There will be times when you shouldn't compromise your core values, your integrity, and you will have the responsibility to speak up in the face of injustice. But listen. Engage. If the other side has a point, learn from them. If they're wrong, rebut them. Teach them. Beat them on the battlefield of ideas. And you might as well start practicing now, because one thing I can guarantee you—you will have to deal with ignorance, hatred, racism, foolishness, trifling folks. (Laughter.) I promise you, you will have to deal with all that at every stage of your life. That may not seem fair, but life has never been completely fair. Nobody promised you a crystal stair. And if you want to make life fair, then you've got to start with the world as it is.

So that's my advice. That's how you change things. Change isn't something that happens every four years or eight years; change is not placing your faith in any particular politician and then just putting your feet up and saying, okay, go. Change is the effort of committed citizens who hitch their wagons to something bigger than themselves and fight for it every single day.

That's what Thurgood Marshall understood—a man who once walked this year, graduated from Howard Law; went home to Baltimore, started his own law practice. He and his mentor, Charles Hamilton Houston, rolled up their sleeves and they set out to overturn segregation. They worked through the NAACP. Filed dozens of lawsuits, fought dozens of cases. And after nearly 20 years of effort—20 years— Thurgood Marshall ultimately succeeded in bringing his righteous cause before the Supreme Court, and securing the ruling in *Brown v. Board of Education* that separate could never be equal. (Applause.) Twenty years.

Marshall, Houston—they knew it would not be easy. They knew it would not be quick. They knew all sorts of obstacles would stand in their way. They knew that even if they won, that would just be the beginning of a longer march to equality. But they had discipline. They had persistence. They had faith—and a sense of humor. And they made life better for all Americans.

And I know you graduates share those qualities. I know it because I've learned about some of the young people graduating here today. There's a young woman named Ciearra Jefferson, who's graduating with you. And I'm just going to use her as an example. I hope you don't mind, Ciearra. Ciearra grew up in Detroit and was raised by a poor single mom who worked seven days a week in an auto plant. And for a time, her family found themselves without a place to call home. They bounced around between friends and family who might take them in. By her senior year,

Ciearra was up at 5:00 a.m. every day, juggling homework, extracurricular activities, volunteering, all while taking care of her little sister. But she knew that education was her ticket to a better life. So she never gave up. Pushed herself to excel. This daughter of a single mom who works on the assembly line turned down a full scholarship to Harvard to come to Howard. (Applause.)

And today, like many of you, Ciearra is the first in her family to graduate from college. And then, she says, she's going to go back to her hometown, just like Thurgood Marshall did, to make sure all the working folks she grew up with have access to the health care they need and deserve. As she puts it, she's going to be a "change agent." She's going to reach back and help folks like her succeed.

And people like Ciearra are why I remain optimistic about America. (Applause.) Young people like you are why I never give in to despair.

James Baldwin once wrote, "Not everything that is faced can be changed, but nothing can be changed until it is faced."

Graduates, each of us is only here because someone else faced down challenges for us. We are only who we are because someone else struggled and sacrificed for us. That's not just Thurgood Marshall's story, or Ciearra's story, or my story, or your story—that is the story of America. A story whispered by slaves in the cotton fields, the song of marchers in Selma, the dream of a King in the shadow of Lincoln. The prayer of immigrants who set out for a new world. The roar of women demanding the vote. The rallying cry of workers who built America. And the GIs who bled overseas for our freedom.

Now it's your turn. And the good news is, you're ready. And when your journey seems too hard, and when you run into a chorus of cynics who tell you that you're being foolish to keep believing or that you can't do something, or that you should just give up, or you should just settle—you might say to yourself a little phrase that I've found handy these last eight years: Yes, we can.

Congratulations, Class of 2016! (Applause.) Good luck! God bless you. God bless the United States of America. I'm proud of you.

Print Citations

CMS: Obama, Barack. "Commencement Address to the Howard University Class of 2016." Speech presented at the Howard University Class of 2016 Commencement, Washington, DC, May, 2016. In *The Reference Shelf: Representative American Speeches 2015-2016*, edited by Betsy Maury, 7-16. Ipswich, MA: H.W. Wilson, 2016.

MLA: Obama, Barack. "Commencement Address to the Howard University Class of 2016." Howard University Class of 2016 Commencement. Washington, DC. May, 2016. Presentation. *The Reference Shelf: Representative American Speeches 2015-2016*. Ed. Betsy Maury. Ipswich: H.W. Wilson, 2016. 7-16. Print.

APA: Obama, B. (2016). Commencement address to the Howard University class of 2016. [Presentation]. *Speech presented at the Howard University Class of 2016 Commencement. Washington, DC.* In Betsy Maury (Ed.), *The reference shelf: Representative American speeches 2015-2016* (pp. 7-16). Ipswich, MA: H.W. Wilson. (Original work published 2016)

In the Future Economy, "We Will Hire Hearts"

By Anne-Marie Slaughter

In this commencement speech given at the University of Utah in 2016, Anne-Marie Slaughter outlines a "principle of three" priorities graduates should keep in mind as they enter into the work world: Care is as Important as Career, Heart is as Important as Head, and Family is as Important as Fame. With these three principles Slaughter shares the wisdom gleaned after many years of research on the issues of work, women and family in modern American life. Anne-Marie Slaughter is currently the president and CEO of New America, a think tank and civic enterprise with offices in Washington and New York. She is also the Bert G. Kerstetter '66 University Professor Emerita of Politics and International Affairs at Princeton University. In 2012 she published the article "Why Women Still Can't Have It All," in the Atlantic, *which quickly became the most read article in the history of the magazine and helped spawn a renewed national debate on the continued obstacles to genuine full male-female equality. She is married to Professor Andrew Moravcsik; they live in Princeton with their two sons.*

So, when I was in college, back when the dinosaurs that you have so many wonderful skeletons of here in Utah roamed the earth, I mastered the rule of three. No matter how complicated the subject I was trying to study, it was always easier to remember it if I broke it into three parts.

So today is a day of emotion and excitement for all of you. You're going to be hearing and thinking and feeling many things. But I hope when it's all done, when you leave, you will remember three very important points.

First, care is as important as career.

In so many ways, college is about career. When you come to college, you come to be educated broadly—what Montaigne referred to as furnishing the back room of your mind.

But you're also preparing for a future career. And for those of you who are graduating today from professional schools and in Ph.D. programs, your time here has been directly about learning the knowledge and acquiring the skills for your career.

What do we mean when we talk about a career? It's a professional journey—one that we hope will ascend or at least allow you to continue learning and growing throughout your life. And it is a way of earning a living. In many ways, your career

Delivered on May 5, 2016 at the University of Utah in Salt Lake City, Utah.

is a lifelong process of investing in yourselves, in the skills, the knowledge and personal growth and development.

Care is investing in others. It is work that is often unpaid. Although, there are also many paid care careers, caring professions like healthcare, teaching or ministry. But care is typically valued far less in our society than the work of your careers.

Women who are lawyers or business people or engineers or in any other profession, when they step back to care for family members or even step out of the workforce often report that they feel they have immediately tumbled in social prestige. They say one minute they're valued for the work they do and the income they bring in and then suddenly they're much less valued. And men who make those choices to defer a promotion, to be the lead parent for their children, not only have their commitment to their careers cast into doubt, they often find their very manhood is questioned.

And yet those choices, those choices to put family first, at least some of the time, are choices that your parents made that were necessary to ensure that all of you are here today getting your degrees.

And some day you are going to have to make the choices to find the time and the love to be able to care for all of them, for the loved ones, the parents and the grandmothers and the other family members who are here so proud to see you graduate today.

So care is vitally important from a social point of view, an economic point of view, indeed even a national security point of view. But care is equally important for all of you—for men as well as for women.

You will grow and learn and develop by investing in others just as much as by investing in yourselves. You will discover a new side of yourself, a side of yourself that takes as much pleasure and pride when others succeed as when you do. The value of investing in others is, of course, well understood by many schools of moral philosophy and great religions, including, of course, the Church of Jesus Christ of Latter-day Saints.

That's the first lesson: Care is as important as career.

The second is that heart is as important as head.

Again, so much of our education is about head. It's about filling all of your heads with the knowledge that you need and the habits of inquiry and intellectual curiosity that will serve you over a lifetime. But many of you, all of you, are going to be pursuing careers in a world in which heart may be the only thing that is not automated.

My friend Dov Seidman, who's a business consultant and a journalist has written that we have moved from the industrial age to the knowledge age or the industrial economy to the knowledge economy, to the human economy.

In the industrial economy, we hired hands. In the knowledge economy, we hire heads. In the human economy, we will hire hearts.

Machines will be increasingly intelligent and, indeed, for those who are in computing science, you know those machines will learn very much the way humans learn. What humans will bring are the traits of our heart—the traits that cannot be programmed into software.

Dov calls them creativity, passion, character and collaboration. I would add compassion and empathy. There's a deeper point here. Dov Seidman is saying that it is heart that is at the core of our humanity.

In the enlightenment, it was head. It was reason ruling the passions. Indeed, think about Descartes: I think, therefore I am. Today, it is feelings and care and empathy and daring that define us. I feel. I think. I dare. I empathize, therefore I am.

And it is interesting to think that we use the word heart to refer both to love and to courage. Love and bravery. Heart matters as much as head.

That message is particularly important for a university. Indeed, a university is a community. And in any community, we learn to put ourselves in each other's shoes and to feel for them and with them. Without those feelings, without that heart, we cannot have reasoned dialogue. We cannot persuade other people unless we ourselves are willing to be persuaded.

This great university has demonstrated that it is a community where reasoned dialogue can take place, where people can reason, talk, grow and change from the heart.

The third and last lesson: Family is as important as fame.

So often we talk about work and family as if they were in eternal tension, pulling at us in opposite directions. And I'll be honest, some of the time it does feel like that, when your child has an earache and it undoes an entire week of meetings.

But none of you would be sitting here without your families. Whether those are your biological families or the people whom you love and love you and support you and whom you choose to make your families. We indeed just heard Charles Koronkowski [the student speaker] say we have become a family.

Family, in its many different incarnations, is not the thing that you have to struggle to make time for as you reach for the stars. Family is the foundation of your ability to thrive.

It was one of my own students who taught me that, who in my office looked at me and she said: "I don't understand constantly this idea that we have to choose between work and family, because without family I couldn't do any of the things that I do."

Family is your foundation. I should also say family keeps you humble, which is valuable, as you go forward. I live with two teenage boys. There is no danger that my head will ever swell.

That lesson that family is just as important as fame is particularly important for the men in the audience. It is men who often still find that their families—their parents, their wives, even their siblings—that their families define their life success in terms of what they do for a living.

Why is that? Why should we expect men to be the constant provider, to stay in the workplace, when perhaps many men would rather provide care rather than cash? Would rather reach a different balance with their life partners to invest in their families as well as in their careers.

One man wrote me that he had left his job when it was clear that the growth potential of his children was greater than the growth potential of his company. And there's nothing wrong with that.

So one more time. Here are the three points, precepts, principles that I hope you will remember: Care is as important as career, heart is as important as head, and family is as important as fame. These are propositions that are particularly relevant for all of you as graduates of this university in this state.

The first inhabitants of this state, the Goshutes, the Shoshone, the Utes, the Paiutes and the Navajos worked hard but lived communally. They cared for each other and for the land.

When the white settlers came, they created a very distinctive diversion of life on the frontier. Utah was not the land of the lone ranger. It was the land of peach-cutting bees, of husking bees, of quilting bees and of barn raisings and many other communal activities. It was a state in which many strong women and men invested in their families as much as in their farms. And in which women got the right to vote in 1870—the second territory to do so, after Wyoming, and before any of the states. In 1870, 50 years before the 19th Amendment.

Utah, as you see on the seal, as you know, is the beehive state. The beehive state for a work ethic that is as communal as it is strong.

So go forth. Hug your loved ones today. Thank them and hold them close to your hearts. Build on this great education and continue to learn and to grow. Strive and struggle and work really hard. But always, always make room for the precious indispensable and priceless work of care.

Thank you very much.

Print Citations

CMS: Slaughter, Anne-Marie. "In the Future Economy 'We Will Hire Hearts.'" Speech presented at the University of Utah Class of 2016 Commencement, May, 2016. In *The Reference Shelf: Representative American Speeches 2015-2016*, edited by Betsy Maury, 18-21. Ipswich, MA: H.W. Wilson, 2016.

MLA: Slaughter, Anne-Marie. "In the Future Economy 'We Will Hire Hearts.'" University of Utah Class of 2016 Commencement. May, 2016. Presentation. *The Reference Shelf: Representative American Speeches 2015-2016.* Ed. Betsy Maury. Ipswich: H.W. Wilson, 2016. 18-21. Print.

APA: Slaughter, A.-M. (2016). In the future economy "We will hire hearts." [Presentation]. *Speech presented at the University of Utah Class of 2016 Commencement.* In Betsy Maury (Ed.), *The reference shelf: Representative American speeches 2015-2016* (pp. 18-21). Ipswich, MA: H.W. Wilson. (Original work published 2016)

Remarks by the First Lady at the
City College of New York Commencement

By Michelle Obama

In the First lady's final commencement address, Michelle Obama emphasized the strength and vitality of public education and celebrated diversity as a key component to intellectual growth. City College, founded in 1847, was the first free public institution of higher education in the United States and boasts more Nobel Prize-winning gradu-ates than any other public institution in the country. Mrs. Obama's speech celebrated the immigrant experience and congratulated graduates on the determination and hard work that it took to succeed here. In an election year that saw immigration become a hotly debated campaign issue, the First Lady applauded the inclusiveness of public universities in helping immigrants achieve the American Dream. Michelle Obama be-came First Lady of the United States in 2008. Before her husband was elected to office, Obama worked for the University of Chicago Medical Center and was a member of the staff of Chicago mayor, Richard M. Daley. As First Lady, Obama has focused on veteran family issues, LGBT rights, girls' access to education, and childhood health.

MRS. OBAMA: Wow! (Applause.) Let me just take it in. First of all, it is beyond a pleasure and an honor to be here to celebrate the City College of New York Class of 2016! You all, I mean, this has been the most fun I think I've had at a commence-ment ever. (Applause.)

Let me just say a few thank yous. Let me start, of course, by thanking President Coico for that wonderful introduction, for her leadership here at City College, for this honorary degree.

I also want to recognize Senator Schumer, Chancellor Milliken, Trustee Shorter, Edward Plotkin, as well as your amazing valedictorian, Antonios Mourdoukoutas —did I get it right? (Applause.) And your amazing salutatorian, Orubba Almansouri. (Applause.) I really don't want to follow those two. (Laughter.) If anybody is won-dering about the quality of education, just listening to those two speakers lets you know what's happening here. And I'm so proud of you both—and to your families, congratulations. Well done. Well done. (Applause.)

And of course, let us not forget Elizabeth Aklilu for her amazing performance of the National Anthem earlier today. She blew it out of the water. (Applause.)

Delivered on June 3, 2016, at City College of New York in New York City.

But most of all, I want to acknowledge all of you– the brilliant, talented, ambitious, accomplished, and all-around outstanding members of the class of 2016! Woo! (Applause.) You give me chills. You all have worked so hard and come so far to reach this milestone, so I know this is a big day for all of you and your families, and for everyone at this school who supported you on this journey.

And in many ways, this is a big day for me too. See, this is my very last commencement address as First Lady of the United States. This is it. (Applause.) So I just want to take it all in. And I think this was the perfect place to be, because this is my last chance to share my love and admiration, and hopefully a little bit of wisdom with a graduating class.

And, graduates, I really want you all to know that there is a reason why, of all of the colleges and universities in this country, I chose this particular school in this particular city for this special moment. (Applause.) And I'm here because of all of you. I mean, we've talked about it—Antonios, I'm going to talk a little bit about diversity, thank you. (Laughter.)

Just look around. Look at who you are. Look at where we're gathered today. As the President eloquently said, at this school, you represent more than 150 nationalities. You speak more than 100 different languages—whoa, just stop there. You represent just about every possible background—every color and culture, every faith and walk of life. And you've taken so many different paths to this moment.

Maybe your family has been in this city for generations, or maybe, like my family, they came to this country centuries ago in chains. Maybe they just arrived here recently, determined to give you a better life.

But, graduates, no matter where your journey started, you have all made it here today through the same combination of unyielding determination, sacrifice, and a whole lot of hard work—commuting hours each day to class, some of you. (Applause.) Yes, amen. (Laughter.) Juggling multiple jobs to support your families and pay your tuition. (Applause.) Studying late into the night, early in the morning; on subways and buses, and in those few precious minutes during breaks at work.

And somehow, you still found time to give back to your communities—tutoring young people, reading to kids, volunteering at hospitals. Somehow, you still managed to do prestigious internships and research fellowships, and join all kinds of clubs and activities. And here at this nationally-ranked university, with a rigorous curriculum and renowned faculty, you rose to the challenge, distinguishing yourselves in your classes, winning countless honors and awards, and getting into top graduate schools across this country. Whoa. (Laughter.)

So, graduates, with your glorious diversity, with your remarkable accomplishments and your deep commitment to your communities, you all embody the very purpose of this school's founding. And, more importantly, you embody the very hopes and dreams carved into the base of that iconic statue not so far from where we sit—on that island where so many of your predecessors at this school first set foot on our shores.

And that is why I wanted to be here today at City College. I wanted to be here to celebrate all of you, this school, this city. (Applause.) Because I know that there is no better way to celebrate this great country than being here with you.

See, all of you know, for centuries, this city has been the gateway to America for so many striving, hope-filled immigrants—folks who left behind everything they knew to seek out this land of opportunity that they dreamed of. And so many of those folks, for them, this school was the gateway to actually realizing that opportunity in their lives, founded on the fundamental truth that talent and ambition know no distinctions of race, nationality, wealth, or fame, and dedicated to the ideals that our Founding Fathers put forth more than two centuries ago: That we are all created equal, all entitled to "life, liberty and the pursuit of happiness." City College became a haven for brilliant, motivated students of every background, a place where they didn't have to hide their last names or their accents, or put on any kind of airs because the students at this school were selected based not on pedigree, but on merit, and merit alone. (Applause.)

So really, it is no accident that this institution has produced 10 Nobel Prize winners—(applause)—along with countless captains of industry, cultural icons, leaders at the highest levels of government. Because talent and effort combined with our various backgrounds and life experiences has always been the lifeblood of our singular American genius.

Just take the example of the great American lyricist, Ira Gershwin, who attended City College a century ago. The son of a Russian-Jewish immigrant, his songs still light up Broadway today. Or consider the story of the former CEO of Intel, Andrew Grove, class of 1960. (Applause.) He was a Hungarian immigrant whose harrowing escape from Nazism and Communism shaped both his talent for business and his commitment to philanthropy.

And just think about the students in this very graduating class—students like the economics and pre-law major from Albania, who also completed the requirements for a philosophy major and dreams of being a public intellectual. The educational theater student from right here in Harlem who's already an award-winning playwright and recently spoke at the White House. The biomedical science major who was born in Afghanistan and plans to be a doctor, a policy maker and an educator. (Applause.) And your salutatorian, whose Yemeni roots inspired her to study Yemini women's writing and to advocate for girls in her community, urging them to find their own voices, to tell their own stories. I could go on.

These are just four of the nearly 4,000 unique and amazing stories in this graduating class—stories that have converged here at City College, this dynamic, inclusive place where you all have had the chance to really get to know each other, to listen to each other's languages, to enjoy each other's food—lasagna, obviously—(laughter)—music, and holidays. Debating each other's ideas, pushing each other to question old assumptions and consider new perspectives.

And those interactions have been such a critical part of your education at this school. Those moments when your classmates showed you that your stubborn opinion wasn't all that well-informed—mmm hmm. (Laughter.) Or when they opened your eyes to an injustice you never knew existed. Or when they helped you with a question that you couldn't have possibly answered on your own.

I think your valedictorian put it best—and this is a quote—he said, "The sole irreplaceable component of my CCNY experience came from learning alongside people with life experiences strikingly different from my own." He said, "I have learned that diversity in human experience gives rise to diversity in thought, which creates distinct ideas and methods of problem solving." That was an okay quote. (Laughter and applause.) Okay, you're bright. (Laughter.) I couldn't have said it better myself.

That is the power of our differences to make us smarter and more creative. And that is how all those infusions of new cultures and ideas, generation after generation, created the matchless alchemy of our melting pot and helped us build the strongest, most vibrant, most prosperous nation on the planet, right here. (Applause.)

But unfortunately, graduates, despite the lessons of our history and the truth of your experience here at City College, some folks out there today seem to have a very different perspective. They seem to view our diversity as a threat to be contained rather than as a resource to be tapped. They tell us to be afraid of those who are different, to be suspicious of those with whom we disagree. They act as if name-calling is an acceptable substitute for thoughtful debate, as if anger and intolerance should be our default state rather than the optimism and openness that have always been the engine of our progress.

But, graduates, I can tell you, as First Lady, I have had the privilege of traveling around the world and visiting dozens of different countries, and I have seen what happens when ideas like these take hold. I have seen how leaders who rule by intimidation—leaders who demonize and dehumanize entire groups of people—often do so because they have nothing else to offer. And I have seen how places that stifle the voices and dismiss the potential of their citizens are diminished; how they are less vital, less hopeful, less free.

Graduates, that is not who we are. That is not what this country stands for. (Applause.) No, here in America, we don't let our differences tear us apart. Not here. Because we know that our greatness comes when we appreciate each other's strengths, when we learn from each other, when we lean on each other. Because in this country, it's never been each person for themselves. No, we're all in this together. We always have been.

And here in America, we don't give in to our fears. We don't build up walls to keep people out because we know that our greatness has always depended on contributions from people who were born elsewhere but sought out this country and made it their home—from innovations like Google and eBay to inventions like the artificial heart, the telephone, even the blue jeans; to beloved patriotic songs like "God Bless America," like national landmarks like the Brooklyn Bridge and, yes, the

White House—both of which were designed by architects who were immigrants. (Applause.)

Finally, graduates, our greatness has never, ever come from sitting back and feeling entitled to what we have. It's never come from folks who climb the ladder of success, or who happen to be born near the top and then pull that ladder up after themselves. No, our greatness has always come from people who expect nothing and take nothing for granted—folks who work hard for what they have then reach back and help others after them.

That is your story, graduates, and that is the story of your families. (Applause.) And it's the story of my family, too. As many of you know, I grew up in a working class family in Chicago. And while neither of my parents went past high school, let me tell you, they saved up every penny that my dad earned at his city job because they were determined to send me to college.

And even after my father was diagnosed with Multiple Sclerosis and he struggled to walk, relying on crutches just to get himself out of bed each morning, my father hardly ever missed a day of work. See, that blue-collar job helped to pay the small portion of my college tuition that wasn't covered by loans or grants or my work-study or my summer jobs. And my dad was so proud to pay that tuition bill on time each month, even taking out loans when he fell short. See, he never wanted me to miss a registration deadline because his check was late. That's my story.

And, graduates, you all have faced challenges far greater than anything I or my family have ever experienced, challenges that most college students could never even imagine. Some of you have been homeless. Some of you have risked the rejection of your families to pursue your education. Many of you have lain awake at night wondering how on Earth you were going to support your parents and your kids and still pay tuition. And many of you know what it's like to live not just month to month or day to day, but meal to meal.

But, graduates, let me tell you, you should never, ever be embarrassed by those struggles. You should never view your challenges as a disadvantage. Instead, it's important for you to understand that your experience facing and overcoming adversity is actually one of your biggest advantages. And I know that because I've seen it myself, not just as a student working my way through school, but years later when I became—before I came to the White House and I worked as a dean at a college.

In that role, I encountered students who had every advantage—their parents paid their full tuition, they lived in beautiful campus dorms. They had every material possession a college kid could want—cars, computers, spending money. But when some of them got their first bad grade, they just fell apart. They lost it, because they were ill-equipped to handle their first encounter with disappointment or falling short.

But, graduates, as you all know, life will put many obstacles in your path that are far worse than a bad grade. You'll have unreasonable bosses and difficult clients and patients. You'll experience illnesses and losses, crises and setbacks that will come out of nowhere and knock you off your feet. But unlike so many other young people, you have already developed the resilience and the maturity that you need to pick yourself up and dust yourself off and keep moving through the pain, keep moving forward. You have developed that muscle. (Applause.)

And with the education you've gotten at this fine school, and the experiences you've had in your lives, let me tell you, nothing—and I mean nothing—is going to stop you from fulfilling your dreams. And you deserve every last one of the successes that I know you will have.

But I also want to be very clear that with those successes comes a set of obligations—to share the lessons you've learned here at this school. The obligation to use the opportunities you've had to help others. That means raising your hand when you get a seat in that board meeting and asking the question, well, whose voices aren't being heard here? What ideas are we missing? It means adding your voice to our national conversation, speaking out for our most cherished values of liberty, opportunity, inclusion, and respect—the values that you've been living here at this school.

It means reaching back to help young people who've been left out and left behind, helping them prepare for college, helping them pay for college, making sure that great public universities like this one have the funding and support that they need. (Applause.) Because we all know that public universities have always been one of the greatest drivers of our prosperity, lifting countless people into the middle class, creating jobs and wealth all across this nation.

Public education is our greatest pathway to opportunity in America. So we need to invest in and strengthen our public universities today, and for generations to come. (Applause.) That is how you will do your part to live up to the oath that you all will take here today—the oath taken by generations of graduates before you to make your city and your world "greater, better, and more beautiful."

More than anything else, graduates, that is the American story. It's your story and the story of those who came before you at this school. It's the story of the son of Polish immigrants named Jonas Salk who toiled for years in a lab until he discovered a vaccine that saved countless lives. It's the story of the son of immigrant—Jamaican immigrants named Colin Powell who became a four-star general, Secretary of State, and a role model for young people across the country.

And, graduates, it's the story that I witness every single day when I wake up in a house that was built by slaves, and I watch my daughters—two beautiful, black young women—head off to school—(applause)—waving goodbye to their father, the President of the United States, the son of a man from Kenya who came here to American—to America for the same reasons as many of you: To get an education and improve his prospects in life.

So, graduates, while I think it's fair to say that our Founding Fathers never could have imagined this day, all of you are very much the fruits of their vision. Their legacy is very much your legacy and your inheritance. And don't let anybody tell you differently. You are the living, breathing proof that the American Dream endures in our time. It's you.

So I want you all to go out there. Be great. Build great lives for yourselves. Enjoy the liberties that you have in this great country. Pursue your own version of happiness. And please, please, always, always do your part to help others do the same.

I love you all. I am so proud of you. (Applause.) Thank you for allowing me to share this final commencement with you. I have so much faith in who you will be. Just keep working hard and keep the faith. I can't wait to see what you all achieve in the years ahead.

Thank you all. God bless. Good luck on the road ahead. (Applause.)

Print Citations

CMS: Obama, Michelle. "Remarks by the First Lady at the City College of New York Commencement." Speech presented at the City College of New York Class of 2016 Commencement, New York, NY, June, 2016. In *The Reference Shelf: Representative American Speeches 2015-2016*, edited by Betsy Maury, 22-28. Ipswich, MA: H.W. Wilson, 2016.

MLA: Obama, Michelle. "Remarks by the First Lady at the City College of New York Commencement." The City College of New York Class of 2016 Commencement. New York, NY. June, 2016. Presentation. *The Reference Shelf: Representative American Speeches 2015-2016*. Ed. Betsy Maury. Ipswich: H.W. Wilson, 2016. 22-28. Print.

APA: Obama, M. (2016). Remarks by the first lady at the City College of New York commencement." [Presentation]. *Speech presented at the City College of New York Class of 2016 Commencement*. New York, NY. In Betsy Maury (Ed.), *The reference shelf: Representative American speeches 2015-2016* (pp. 22-28). Ipswich, MA: H.W. Wilson. (Original work published 2016)

Now, We Are All Founders

By Leah Busque

Sweet Briar College in Sweet Briar, Virginia was founded in 1901 as a private women's liberal arts college. In 2015 it had a dramatic and tumultuous year, nearly closing its doors due to financial insolvency. Through the efforts of alumnae, parents, faculty, and other friends of the College it was saved from closure and emerged stronger with an incredibly engaged community supporting its mission into the future. In this address to the first graduating class since the threat of closure in July of 2015, Leah Busque tells graduates that they are all founders and gives advice about knowing their own founding stories, having audacious goals, and being engaged in the world. Busque graduated from Sweet Briar College in 2001, earning a Bachelor of Science in Mathematics and Computer Science. She is an American entrepreneur who founded TaskRabbit, an online and mobile marketplace that allows users to outsource small jobs and tasks to others in their neighborhood.

We all sit here today, together, after an absolutely epic year. A year that has tested our resilience, perseverance, and strength as a community. We come together today to celebrate our historic success, to recognize the challenges we have overcome, and to boldly move forward into a bright future.

To the faculty, staff, and administration who have been in the trenches here daily, who have made this year not only possible, but have made it a high quality, culturally rich, educationally exceptional experience, I commend and celebrate you.

To the parents—my goodness. You all are heroes. Thank you for believing in this institution, thank you for trusting us with your most precious and important cargo—your daughters. Your support will always be revered.

There are many others throughout the broad Sweet Briar community who allow us all to sit here today—thank you to all of you who have been a part of this momentous year, thank you for ensuring that we are here today to celebrate the Class of 2016.

Now, We Are All Founders

Sweet Briar has offered us all a very special, very unique gift: what could be the most important leadership lesson many of us will ever tackle. This experience has given us all an opportunity to step up in a way that we wouldn't have before. The

Delivered at Sweet Briar College on May 14, 2016 in Sweet Briar, Virginia.

opportunity to examine our core values, to take control of our future, to prove that the impossible is just another problem to solve.

Ultimately, because of this experience, we have earned the right to crown ourselves with a new title, a new identity, a new piece of our being that we may not have even known was inside us. Now, we are all Founders. The faculty, staff, administration, alums, parents, community …. and especially this historic Class of 2016: We are all Founders now.

In 1906, the college opened with 51 women: the pioneers of their day. They were the first founding class. 110 years later, we celebrate 82 women who have boldly chosen to take a stand to renew this institution. You are the second founding class, following in the footsteps of our original Founder, Indiana Fletcher Williams. This class declares that education dedicated to women is relevant and important.

As the founding class for the next century of women, you have earned, as we call it in Silicon Valley, your "Founder's Badge." Welcome to this very exclusive, very elite club. This is a club you can't buy your way into. It's not something you can slowly work your way up to. Being a Founder is something that you experience, something that you own, something that you earn. You all have made sacrifices and taken risks, and you have the battle scars to prove it. You've plowed ahead, regardless of whether what's around the corner is the highest of highs or the lowest of lows.

It's imperative that we all recognize and celebrate the giant leap of faith you took to ensure this founding class graduates today. Now, we are all Founders.

I am so glad my parents and family could join me here today. It's been almost twenty years since my mom and I made the 12-hour drive down from Boston for Accepted Applicants weekend. I remember everything about it, especially those tense moments maneuvering the rental car through the Blue Ridge Mountains, the twists and turns of Route 60. I remember looking at my mom and thinking, *we are not in Boston anymore.*

But as soon as we turned into campus and drove up that gorgeous tree-lined drive, surrounded by meadows, and forests, and even deer! I knew. I knew this is what I wanted my college experience to look like and feel like. This was where I belonged. Where I *belong.* My daughter is here as well—Congratulations Class of 2035!—and I can't wait until she is old enough to understand this dramatic story of heroism, activism, and achievement. I will tell her about my home on these 3,300 acres and these 82 female founders who came back to their school and paved the way for her to be here. And I will try very hard to convince her that there are more students than deer.

In 2008 I founded my own business. I was 7 years out of Sweet Briar, working at IBM as a computer programmer, and I really had no idea what I was getting myself into. (Honestly, sometimes I still don't feel like I know what I'm doing. Don't tell my investors.) Today, I want to share with you three lessons, I happened to learn as a Founder. Trust me when I tell you that these lessons are pertinent no matter who you are, what your passions are, or where life takes you.

Lesson #1: Know Your Founding story

Lesson #1: Know your founding story. Because you're a founder now, you must have a founding story. Lucky for you: you saved your college. That's not a bad start for a founding story! But now you have to craft it. You have to apply it to who you are, what inspires you, and what you believe in. You can use it to propel you forward.

This is a story that you will tell about a trillion times, to every single person you meet. Friends. Family. Employers. Mentors. Investors. Advisors. On job interviews. People sitting next you to on the bus. You will be able to recite this story, perfectly from memory, every time in the same exact way. You will get sick of hearing yourself tell this story, and you will love it.

Every good founding story has 3 parts—(1) A personal back drop, (2) A moment of inspiration, and (3) an innovative path forward.

My founding story started 8 years ago during a cold, winter night in Boston. It was 2008. My husband, Kevin, and I were sitting in our kitchen, getting ready to go out to dinner, when we realized we were out of dog food. Kevin is also in technology, so we always had these very geeky conversations in the house. That night, it turned into …

(that was my personal backdrop)

… wouldn't it be nice if there was a place online we could go, say we needed dog food, name the price we were willing to pay? We were certain there was someone in our own neighborhood that would be willing to help us out, maybe even someone at the store at that very second, it was just a matter of connecting with them.

(that was my moment of inspiration)

Now this was 2008. The dark ages. The iPhone had just come out, no one was utilizing location-based technologies yet, and Facebook was just emerging out of the college scene. (Yes, I was at SBC without Facebook!!). But as a technologist myself, I became passionate about merging together these three technologies—social networking, mobile technologies, and location awareness, to connect real people in the real world, to get real things done. Now, we're even doing it in real time!

(that was my innovative path forward)

Eight years later, my company TaskRabbit has raised $50 million from top tier Silicon Valley Investors, expanded into 20 cities across the country, opened an international market in London, and helped define an industry widely known as the Sharing Economy. It all started on that cold winter night in Boston. That is my founding story.

Think about what your founding story is and how this past year at Sweet Briar has shaped that story for you. Get clarity around this story and be ready to shout it from the rooftops. This is the gift that SBC has given you: concrete proof that you are tenacious, you are mission-driven, and you will persevere. Make no mistake: this is rare for anyone, especially a woman of your age. This is a tremendous asset, so use it. You have proven yourself today more than any other graduating class in history. When people hear your founding story, they will commend you, reward you, and want you to be a part of their team. Most important: they will want you to lead. Go out and use this story to show the world what a force you can be!

And oh yeah, Kobe, our dog, did get to eat that night. We gave him some extra treats in his bowl and he was happy.

Lesson # 2: Have Big Hairy Audacious Goals, but Take Baby Steps

Lesson #2: I want you to have Big Hairy Audacious Goals … BHAGs. BHAGs are the kind of goals that are so outrageous, so ambitious, that it is almost crazy to consider them. I picture these goals like one of the characters from that book *Where the Wild Things Are*: patchy purple fur, a large green, troll like nose, and bright yellow eyes. This beast wears a giant golden crown as she tromps around the jungle, blazing everything in her path.

You may feel compelled to keep this beast hidden in your closet; you may not even dare to whisper the crazy ambitions of this outrageous animal. But if it makes you uncomfortable, you're on the right track. If people think you're crazy, unrealistic, or too ambitious, that's when you know you are aiming high enough.

At IBM, my team was made up of predominantly men, and I was easily the youngest by about 20 years. I remember vividly the day that I was told I was "too ambitious" by a teammate. I thought "too ambitious" … Is that a thing? He said it as if having ambition was a *negative* thing. I was perplexed. Confused. Befuddled, even. Years later I realize, it is a well-studied phenomenon that men are celebrated for their ambition, while women are judged negatively for it, because it violates communal stereotypes.

That was a wake up call! Not everyone has or appreciates ambition. When I founded a company of my own, I knew I would always challenge my team to have ambitious goals.

One brainstorming session, early on at TaskRabbit … we challenged ourselves to come up with one BHAG we wanted to achieve. What was something so outrageous that we all might laugh when we put it up on the white board? Someone said, when President Obama posts a Task on TaskRabbit, that would be a great BHAG. And yes, we laughed. All of us.

Well, fast forward a few years, we have been invited to the White House multiple times, presented TaskRabbit to President Obama, and partnered with their Disaster Relief Team to offer our technology in times of crisis. President Obama has seen the app with his own eyes, and although he hasn't technically posted a Task on TaskRabbit himself… many of his closest advisers have! So, I'm calling that a win. Besides, in eight months he's going to have a lot of free time on his hands. Maybe he'll start delivering groceries.

How many people thought saving Sweet Briar was too ambitious? That raising $21 million dollars in 90 days would be too crazy? That it couldn't be done. And yet … here we all are! Proof that you don't mess with the Vixens!

But the truth is that while Sweet Briar has been saved, the work here is not done. We must continue to push forward so that this place can thrive for the next century of women.

I have a goal for this institution to be *the* premier women's college in the country. Known for launching exceptional global leaders into the world.

I have a goal for women to achieve equal pay across all industries in this country in my lifetime.

I have a goal to fix the "pipeline problem" of not enough female engineers in the technology industry.

I have a big hairy audacious goal for TaskRabbit to achieve intergalactic domination. Not just this galaxy … all the galaxies.

But I'm not the only one with BHAGs. Mark Zuckerberg wants to make sure affordable access to basic Internet services are available to every person in the world.

Malala Yousafzai wants every girl (even if they are living in a war-torn country or surviving a refugee camp) to have access to 12 years of free, safe, quality primary and secondary education.

Now the key with these BHAGs, the same key to dealing with any purple-furred, troll-nosed beast, is: Don't let them control you. The only way to tame them is to be realistic about what that process entails. I don't wake up every morning and tackle revolutionizing work around the globe. I think: What can I do in the next 24 hours to move my business forward? Sure, tomorrow that could mean briefing the President on how TaskRabbit's technology can help in a time of crisis. But maybe today that means taking out the trash. And that's okay! You have to start somewhere. Dare to dream, yes, but make sure your dreams can be broken down into actionable pieces.

Oh, and also… It's never a straight path from upstart to intergalactic domination. You are going to fail. If your goals are big enough, you're *supposed* to fail. It's what you learn from these failures that will push you closer towards your goals. Embrace the idea of working your way up from the bottom, taking baby steps toward your goals, and be okay with failing … just remember to learn something every single day that will help move you forward.

So embrace those good-natured beasts that live inside of you. Keep your eye on them. Nurture them. Take small steps, every day, toward them. Live deliberately to carry out the vision for your life. Embrace those big hairy audacious goals and unleash them into the world.

Lesson #3: Be Engaged in the World

Lesson #3: Be engaged in the world. Now, I'm going to let you in on a little secret. When I had the idea for TaskRabbit that cold winter night, I had already spent many months deliberately training myself to be in an entrepreneurial mindset. Frankly, I was getting bored at IBM and hungry for new ways of thinking and working. Task-Rabbit was not the first idea I had thought about pursuing. My founding story is always told as a moment of inspiration, and it truly was, but it was also the many months leading up to that moment that prepared me to be open to this inspiration. I had to first be in that entrepreneurial mindset, and that is the less glamorous truth.

Thinking this way is not just for tech inventors and builders. It will serve you well across many aspect of your life, no matter what your aspirations are. But how can you skip years of wasted time and energy being on autopilot and train yourself to think entrepreneurially? A good friend of mine, Adam Grant, recently published a fantastic book called *Originals*. In it, he explores how everyone can be an original thinker and what makes for a successful entrepreneurial mindset. One of my favorite parts in his book is the concept of Vu Ja De, which is the opposite of De Ja Vu. You know that feeling you get when you've experienced something before, but in reality its really the first time you've ever seen it? We've all had that feeling. It can be explained as a simple glitch in the Matrix. Adam's concept of Vu Ja De is the opposite of this. It is being able to look at the same thing hundreds of times, but have the ability to see it differently. It's having a familiar experience, something you do all the time, but training yourself, your mind, to look at it from a different angle.

My Vu Ja De moment was when Kevin and I ran out of dog food that cold winter night. It wasn't the first time we had run out of dog food. Poor Kobe had experienced this with our delinquent parenting before, though all 100 pounds of him proved we kept him very well fed! We could have just moved on, like every other time. We could have cooked Kobe a nice bowl of boiled chicken and rice, and gone out the next morning to retrieve his dog food. But for the first time, we deliberately decided to look at the problem differently. We actively refrained from going on autopilot and forced, what turned out to be an exciting conversation on what was possible. At that moment of Vu Ja De, it all came together. Four months later I had quit my job at IBM to build the first version of the site, and the rest, is as they say, history.

So be engaged in the world. Embrace every moment of would-be inspiration. Look for Vu Ja De moments. Train your entrepreneurial mindset and be open to these inspirational moments. Because as a Founder now, you can have a real impact on the world—large and small. You all can.

And there you have it. Three life lessons: Find your founding story. Establish big hairy audacious goals. Be engaged in the world around you. It's as simple as that!

I mentioned earlier that you are part of a very exclusive, very elite club. This is true. All of you are part of this—parents, professors, administrators, the entire community. Now, we are all Founders. What is also true, particularly for this very special graduating class, is that as a female founder, you are part of an even smaller, even more elite club. You will consistently be in the minority for many of the paths that you follow. There just aren't enough of us out there yet, but the numbers are changing, and your induction into this special club only helps those numbers.

Nevertheless, there will be roadblocks. There will be inequalities. Your ambition will be criticized. And you will be underestimated. Constantly. This can end up being a tremendous advantage for you! Most of the world will not see you coming, and that is a brilliant thing. You will stand out and capture the spotlight in a way that people may not expect. You will surprise them. Heck, you may even surprise yourself sometimes. Focus on following your story. Ignore the noise. Never worry if you are good enough to do something, know you are, and always act like it. Embrace that confidence that Sweet Briar has instilled in you. I know it's there. I'm living proof.

Being here today with you has been such an incredible honor, a moment I will always cherish and remember. You all are truly an inspiration to me. Seeing you ready to go out and blaze your own paths in the world, particularly after the year that we've all had together. It really is special. For the rest of your lives, people will look up to you for being the most important kind of founder. Because if there's one thing harder than building an institution, it's rebuilding it, and we will, because we are all Founders now.

Print Citations

CMS: Busque, Leah. "Now We Are All Founders." Speech presented at the Sweet Briar College Class of 2016 Commencement, Sweet Briar, Virginia, May, 2016. In *The Reference Shelf: Representative American Speeches 2015-2016*, edited by Betsy Maury, 29-35. Ipswich, MA: H.W. Wilson, 2016.

MLA: Busque, Leah. "Now We Are All Founders." Sweet Briar College. Sweet Briar Class of 2016 Commencement, Virginia. May, 2016. Presentation. *The Reference Shelf: Representative American Speeches 2015-2016*. Ed. Betsy Maury. Ipswich: H.W. Wilson, 2016. 29-35. Print.

APA: Busque, Leah. (2016). Now we are all founders. [Presentation]. *Speech presented at the Sweet Briar College Class of 2016 Commencement.* Sweet Briar, Virginia. In Betsy Maury (Ed.), *The reference shelf: Representative American speeches 2015-2016* (pp. 29-35). Ipswich, MA: H.W. Wilson. (Original work published 2016)

The Mistrust of Science

By Atul Gawande

In this speech, Dr. Gawande urges students to adhere to the rigors of scientific inquiry in explaining the world around them. He encourages graduates to become part of the scientific community, the most powerful collective enterprise in human history. By applying scientific inquiry to the world around them, graduates not only connect with forbearers who delved into serious questions of the universe, they become trusted sources of knowledge for future generations. Atul Gawande, MD, MPH, is a surgeon, writer, and public health researcher. He practices general and endocrine surgery at Brigham and Women's Hospital. He is a professor in the Department of Health Policy and Management at the Harvard T.H. Chan School of Public Health and the Samuel O. Thier Professor of Surgery at Harvard Medical School. He is also executive director of Ariadne Labs, a joint center for health systems innovation, and chairman of Lifebox, a nonprofit organization making surgery safer globally. Dr. Gawande has been a staff writer for the New Yorker *magazine since 1998 and has written four* New York Times *bestsellers:* Complications, Better, The Checklist Manifesto, *and most recently,* Being Mortal: Medicine *and* What Matters in the End.

If this place has done its job—and I suspect it has—you're all scientists now. Sorry, English and history graduates, even you are, too. Science is not a major or a career. It is a commitment to a systematic way of thinking, an allegiance to a way of building knowledge and explaining the universe through testing and factual observation. The thing is, that isn't a normal way of thinking. It is unnatural and counterintuitive. It has to be learned. Scientific explanation stands in contrast to the wisdom of divinity and experience and common sense. Common sense once told us that the sun moves across the sky and that being out in the cold produced colds. But a scientific mind recognized that these intuitions were only hypotheses. They had to be tested.

When I came to college from my Ohio home town, the most intellectually unnerving thing I discovered was how wrong many of my assumptions were about how the world works—whether the natural or the human-made world. I looked to my professors and fellow-students to supply my replacement ideas. Then I returned home with some of those ideas and told my parents everything they'd got wrong (which they just loved). But, even then, I was just replacing one set of received beliefs for another. It took me a long time to recognize the particular mind-set that scientists have. The great physicist Edwin Hubble, speaking at Caltech's commencement in 1938, said a scientist has "a healthy skepticism, suspended judgment, and

Delivered at California Institute of Technology on June 10, 2016 in Pasadena, California.

36

disciplined imagination"—not only about other people's ideas but also about his or her own. The scientist has an experimental mind, not a litigious one.

As a student, this seemed to me more than a way of thinking. It was a way of being—a weird way of being. You are supposed to have skepticism and imagination, but not too much. You are supposed to suspend judgment, yet exercise it. Ultimately, you hope to observe the world with an open mind, gathering facts and testing your predictions and expectations against them. Then you make up your mind and either affirm or reject the ideas at hand. But you also hope to accept that nothing is ever completely settled, that all knowledge is just probable knowledge. A contradictory piece of evidence can always emerge. Hubble said it best when he said, "The scientist explains the world by successive approximations."

The scientific orientation has proved immensely powerful. It has allowed us to nearly double our lifespan during the past century, to increase our global abundance, and to deepen our understanding of the nature of the universe. Yet scientific knowledge is not necessarily trusted. Partly, that's because it is incomplete. But even where the knowledge provided by science is overwhelming, people often resist it—sometimes outright deny it. Many people continue to believe, for instance, despite massive evidence to the contrary, that childhood vaccines cause autism (they do not); that people are safer owning a gun (they are not); that genetically modified crops are harmful (on balance, they have been beneficial); that climate change is not happening (it is).

Vaccine fears, for example, have persisted despite decades of research showing them to be unfounded. Some twenty-five years ago, a statistical analysis suggested a possible association between autism and thimerosal, a preservative used in vaccines to prevent bacterial contamination. The analysis turned out to be flawed, but fears took hold. Scientists then carried out hundreds of studies, and *found no link. Still, fears persisted.* Countries removed the preservative but experienced no reduction in autism—yet fears grew. A British study claimed a connection between the onset of autism in eight children and the timing of their vaccinations for measles, mumps, and rubella. That paper was retracted due to findings of fraud: the lead author had falsified and misrepresented the data on the children. Repeated efforts to confirm the findings were unsuccessful. Nonetheless, vaccine rates plunged, leading to *outbreaks of measles and mumps* that, last year, sickened tens of thousands of children across the U.S., Canada, and Europe, and resulted in deaths.

People are prone to resist scientific claims when they clash with intuitive beliefs. They don't see measles or mumps around anymore. They do see children with autism. And they see a mom who says, "My child was perfectly fine until he got a vaccine and became autistic."

Now, you can tell them that correlation is not causation. You can say that children get a vaccine every two to three months for the first couple years of their life, so the onset of any illness is bound to follow vaccination for many kids. You can say that the science shows no connection. But once an idea has got embedded and become widespread, it becomes very difficult to dig it out of people's brains—especially when they do not trust scientific authorities. And we are experiencing a significant decline in trust in scientific authorities.

The sociologist Gordon Gauchat studied US survey data from 1974 to 2010 and found some *deeply alarming trends*. Despite increasing education levels, the public's trust in the scientific community has been decreasing. This is particularly true among conservatives, even educated conservatives. In 1974, conservatives with college degrees had the highest level of trust in science and the scientific community. Today, they have the lowest.

Today, we have multiple factions putting themselves forward as what Gauchat describes as their own cultural domains, "generating their own knowledge base that is often in conflict with the cultural authority of the scientific community." Some are religious groups (challenging evolution, for instance). Some are industry groups (as with climate skepticism). Others tilt more to the left (such as those that reject the medical establishment). As varied as these groups are, they are all alike in one way. They all harbor sacred beliefs that they do not consider open to question.

To defend those beliefs, few dismiss the authority of science. They dismiss the authority of the scientific community. People don't argue back by claiming divine authority anymore. They argue back by claiming to have the truer scientific authority. It can make matters incredibly confusing. You have to be able to recognize the difference between claims of science and those of pseudoscience.

Science's defenders have identified five hallmark moves of pseudoscientists. They argue that the scientific consensus emerges from a conspiracy to suppress dissenting views. They produce fake experts, who have views contrary to established knowledge but do not actually have a credible scientific track record. They cherry-pick the data and papers that challenge the dominant view as a means of discrediting an entire field. They deploy false analogies and other logical fallacies. And they set impossible expectations of research: when scientists produce one level of certainty, the pseudoscientists insist they achieve another.

It's not that some of these approaches never provide valid arguments. Sometimes an analogy *is* useful, or higher levels of certainty *are* required. But when you see several or all of these tactics deployed, you know that you're not dealing with a scientific claim anymore. Pseudoscience is the form of science without the substance.

The challenge of what to do about this—how to defend science as a more valid approach to explaining the world—has actually been addressed by science itself. Scientists have done experiments. In 2011, two Australian researchers compiled many of the findings in *The Debunking Handbook*. The results are sobering. The evidence is that rebutting bad science doesn't work; in fact, it commonly backfires. Describing facts that contradict an unscientific belief actually spreads familiarity with the belief and strengthens the conviction of believers. That's just the way the brain operates; misinformation sticks, in part because it gets incorporated into a person's mental model of how the world works. Stripping out the misinformation therefore fails, because it threatens to leave a painful gap in that mental model—or no model at all.

So, then, what is a science believer to do? Is the future just an unending battle of warring claims? Not necessarily. Emerging from the findings was also evidence that suggested how you might build trust in science. Rebutting bad science may not be effective, but asserting the true facts of good science is. And including the narrative that explains them is even better. You don't focus on what's wrong with the vaccine myths, for instance. Instead, you point out: giving children vaccines has proved far safer than not. How do we know? Because of a massive body of evidence, including the fact that we've tried the alternate experiment before. Between 1989 and 1991, vaccination among poor urban children in the US dropped. And the result was fifty-five thousand cases of measles and a hundred and twenty-three deaths.

The other important thing is to expose the bad science tactics that are being used to mislead people. Bad science has a pattern, and helping people recognize the pattern arms them to come to more scientific beliefs themselves. Having a scientific understanding of the world is fundamentally about how you judge which information to trust. It doesn't mean poring through the evidence on every question yourself. You can't. Knowledge has become too vast and complex for any one person, scientist or otherwise, to convincingly master more than corners of it.

Few working scientists can give a ground-up explanation of the phenomenon they study; they rely on information and techniques borrowed from other scientists. Knowledge and the virtues of the scientific orientation live far more in the community than the individual. When we talk of a "scientific community," we are pointing to something critical: that advanced science is a social enterprise, characterized by an intricate division of cognitive labor. Individual scientists, no less than the quacks, can be famously bull-headed, overly enamored of pet theories, dismissive of new evidence, and heedless of their fallibility. (Hence Max Planck's observation that science advances one funeral at a time.) But as a community endeavor, it is beautifully self-correcting.

Beautifully organized, however, it is not. Seen up close, the scientific community—with its muddled peer-review process, badly written journal articles, subtly contemptuous letters to the editor, overtly contemptuous subreddit threads, and pompous pronouncements of the academy—looks like a rickety vehicle for getting to the truth. Yet the hive mind swarms ever forward. It now advances knowledge in almost every realm of existence—even the humanities, where neuroscience and computerization are shaping understanding of everything from free will to how art and literature have evolved over time.

Today, you become part of the scientific community, arguably the most powerful collective enterprise in human history. In doing so, you also inherit a role in explaining it and helping it reclaim territory of trust at a time when that territory has been shrinking. In my clinic and my work in public health, I regularly encounter people who are deeply skeptical of even the most basic knowledge established by what journalists label "mainstream" science (as if the other thing is anything like science)—whether it's facts about physiology, nutrition, disease, medicines, you name it. The doubting is usually among my most, not least, educated patients. Education may expose people to science, but it has a *countervailing effect* as well, leading people to be more individualistic and ideological.

The mistake, then, is to believe that the educational credentials you get today give you any special authority on truth. What you have gained is far more important: an understanding of what real truth-seeking looks like. It is the effort not of a single person but of a group of people—the bigger the better—pursuing ideas with curiosity, inquisitiveness, openness, and discipline. As scientists, in other words.

Even more than what you think, how you think matters. The stakes for understanding this could not be higher than they are today, because we are not just battling for what it means to be scientists. We are battling for what it means to be citizens.

Print Citations

CMS: Gawande, Atul. "The Mistrust of Science." Speech presented at the California Institute of Technology Class of 2016 Commencement, June, 2016. In *The Reference Shelf: Representative American Speeches 2015-2016*, edited by Betsy Maury, 36-40. Ipswich, MA: H.W. Wilson, 2016.

MLA: Gawande, Atul. "The Mistrust of Science." California Institute of Technology Class of 2016 Commencement. June, 2016. Presentation. *The Reference Shelf: Representative American Speeches 2015-2016*. Ed. Betsy Maury. Ipswich: H.W. Wilson, 2016. 36-40. Print.

APA: Gawande, A. (2016). The mistrust of science. [Presentation]. *Speech presented at the California Institute of Technology Class of 2016 Commencement.* In Betsy Maury (Ed.), *The reference shelf: Representative American speeches 2015-2016* (pp. 36-40). Ipswich, MA: H.W. Wilson. (Original work published 2016)

2
Campaign Speeches

Tasos Katopodis/WireImage

Peter Thiel speaks on the fourth day of the Republican National Convention on July 21, 2016 at the Quicken Loans Arena in Cleveland, Ohio.

Remarks by the First Lady at the Democratic National Convention

By Michelle Obama

In what was hailed as one of the best speeches of the Democratic National Convention in 2016 and one of the First Lady's own best speeches, Michelle Obama's short but affecting remarks set a hopeful tone on the opening night of the convention. Mrs. Obama spoke to voters as a parent and framed the presidential election as a choice voters must make about who would have the power to shape the children of America. She asked voters to think about the president as someone who would be charged with leaving something better for the nation's next generation, a leader who is worthy of the promise and impossibly big dreams all Americans have for their children. Michelle Obama became First Lady of the United States in 2008. Before her husband was elected to office, Obama worked for the University of Chicago Medical Center and was a member of the staff of Chicago mayor, Richard M. Daley. As First Lady, Obama has focused on veteran family issues, LGBT rights, girls' access to education, and childhood health.

MRS. OBAMA: Thank you all. (Applause.) Thank you so much. You know, it's hard to believe that it has been eight years since I first came to this convention to talk with you about why I thought my husband should be President. (Applause.) Remember how I told you about his character and conviction, his decency and his grace—the traits that we've seen every day that he's served our country in the White House.

I also told you about our daughters—how they are the heart of our hearts, the center of our world. And during our time in the White House, we've had the joy of watching them grow from bubbly little girls into poised young women—a journey that started soon after we arrived in Washington, when they set off for their first day at their new school.

I will never forget that winter morning as I watched our girls, just seven and ten years old, pile into those black SUVs with all those big men with guns. (Laughter.) And I saw their little faces pressed up against the window, and the only thing I could think was, "What have we done?" (Laughter.) See, because at that moment, I realized that our time in the White House would form the foundation for who they would become, and how well we managed this experience could truly make or break them.

Delivered at the Democratic National Convention on July 25, 2016 at the Wells Fargo Center, Philadelphia, Pennsylvania

That is what Barack and I think about every day as we try to guide and protect our girls through the challenges of this unusual life in the spotlight—how we urge them to ignore those who question their father's citizenship or faith. (Applause.) How we insist that the hateful language they hear from public figures on TV does not represent the true spirit of this country. (Applause.) How we explain that when someone is cruel, or acts like a bully, you don't stoop to their level—no, our motto is, when they go low, we go high. (Applause.)

With every word we utter, with every action we take, we know our kids are watching us. We as parents are their most important role models. And let me tell you, Barack and I take that same approach to our jobs as President and First Lady, because we know that our words and actions matter not just to our girls, but to children across this country—kids who tell us, "I saw you on TV, I wrote a report on you for school." Kids like the little black boy who looked up at my husband, his eyes wide with hope, and he wondered, "Is my hair like yours?" (Applause.)

And make no mistake about it, this November, when we go to the polls, that is what we're deciding—not Democrat or Republican, not left or right. No, this election, and every election, is about who will have the power to shape our children for the next four or eight years of their lives. (Applause.) And I am here tonight because in this election, there is only one person who I trust with that responsibility, only one person who I believe is truly qualified to be President of the United States, and that is our friend, Hillary Clinton. (Applause.)

See, I trust Hillary to lead this country because I've seen her lifelong devotion to our nation's children—not just her own daughter, who she has raised to perfection—(applause)—but every child who needs a champion: Kids who take the long way to school to avoid the gangs. Kids who wonder how they'll ever afford college. Kids whose parents don't speak a word of English but dream of a better life. Kids who look to us to determine who and what they can be.

You see, Hillary has spent decades doing the relentless, thankless work to actually make a difference in their lives—(applause)—advocating for kids with disabilities as a young lawyer. Fighting for children's health care as First Lady and for quality child care in the Senate. And when she didn't win the nomination eight years ago, she didn't get angry or disillusioned. (Applause.) Hillary did not pack up and go home. Because as a true public servant, Hillary knows that this is so much bigger than her own desires and disappointments. (Applause.) So she proudly stepped up to serve our country once again as Secretary of State, traveling the globe to keep our kids safe.

And look, there were plenty of moments when Hillary could have decided that this work was too hard, that the price of public service was too high, that she was tired of being picked apart for how she looks or how she talks or even how she laughs. But here's the thing—what I admire most about Hillary is that she never buckles under pressure. (Applause.) She never takes the easy way out. And Hillary Clinton has never quit on anything in her life. (Applause.)

And when I think about the kind of President that I want for my girls and all our children, that's what I want. I want someone with the proven strength to persevere.

Someone who knows this job and takes it seriously. Someone who understands that the issues a President faces are not black and white and cannot be boiled down to 140 characters. (Applause.) Because when you have the nuclear codes at your fingertips and the military in your command, you can't make snap decisions. You can't have a thin skin or a tendency to lash out. You need to be steady, and measured, and well-informed. (Applause.)

I want a President with a record of public service, someone whose life's work shows our children that we don't chase fame and fortune for ourselves, we fight to give everyone a chance to succeed—(applause)—and we give back, even when we're struggling ourselves, because we know that there is always someone worse off, and there but for the grace of God go I. (Applause.)

I want a President who will teach our children that everyone in this country matters—a President who truly believes in the vision that our founders put forth all those years ago: That we are all created equal, each a beloved part of the great American story. (Applause.) And when crisis hits, we don't turn against each other—no, we listen to each other. We lean on each other. Because we are always stronger together. (Applause.)

And I am here tonight because I know that that is the kind of president that Hillary Clinton will be. And that's why, in this election, I'm with her. (Applause.)

You see, Hillary understands that the President is about one thing and one thing only—it's about leaving something better for our kids. That's how we've always moved this country forward—by all of us coming together on behalf of our children—folks who volunteer to coach that team, to teach that Sunday school class because they know it takes a village. Heroes of every color and creed who wear the uniform and risk their lives to keep passing down those blessings of liberty.

Police officers and protestors in Dallas who all desperately want to keep our children safe. (Applause.) People who lined up in Orlando to donate blood because it could have been their son, their daughter in that club. (Applause.) Leaders like Tim Kaine—(applause)—who show our kids what decency and devotion look like. Leaders like Hillary Clinton, who has the guts and the grace to keep coming back and putting those cracks in that highest and hardest glass ceiling until she finally breaks through, lifting all of us along with her. (Applause.)

That is the story of this country, the story that has brought me to this stage tonight, the story of generations of people who felt the lash of bondage, the shame of servitude, the sting of segregation, but who kept on striving and hoping and doing what needed to be done so that today, I wake up every morning in a house that was built by slaves—(applause)—and I watch my daughters—two beautiful, intelligent, black young women—playing with their dogs on the White House lawn. (Applause.) And because of Hillary Clinton, my daughters—and all our sons and daughters—now take for granted that a woman can be President of the United States. (Applause.)

So don't let anyone ever tell you that this country isn't great, that somehow we need to make it great again. Because this, right now, is the greatest country on earth. (Applause.) And as my daughters prepare to set out into the world, I want a leader who is worthy of that truth, a leader who is worthy of my girls' promise and all our kids' promise, a leader who will be guided every day by the love and hope and impossibly big dreams that we all have for our children.

So in this election, we cannot sit back and hope that everything works out for the best. We cannot afford to be tired, or frustrated, or cynical. No, hear me—between now and November, we need to do what we did eight years ago and four years ago: We need to knock on every door. We need to get out every vote. We need to pour every last ounce of our passion and our strength and our love for this country into electing Hillary Clinton as President of the United States of America.

Let's get to work. Thank you all, and God bless.

Print Citations

CMS: Obama, Michelle. "Remarks by the First Lady at the Democratic National Convention." Speech presented at the Wells Fargo Center, Philadelphia, PA, July, 2016. In *The Reference Shelf: Representative American Speeches 2015-2016*, edited by Betsy Maury, 43-46. Ipswich, MA: H.W. Wilson, 2016.

MLA: Obama, Michelle. "Remarks by the First Lady at the Democratic National Convention." Wells Fargo Center. Philadelphia, PA. July, 2016. Presentation. *The Reference Shelf: Representative American Speeches 2015-2016.* Ed. Betsy Maury. Ipswich: H.W. Wilson, 2016. 43-46. Print.

APA: Obama, M. (2016). Remarks by the first lady at the democratic national convention. [Presentation]. *Speech presented at the Wells Fargo Center.* Philadelphia, PA. In Betsy Maury (Ed.), *The reference shelf: Representative American speeches 2015-2016* (pp. 43-46). Ipswich, MA: H.W. Wilson. (Original work published 2016)

Former Attorney General Addresses the 2016 Democratic National Convention

By Eric Holder

At the Democratic National Convention former Attorney General Eric Holder whole-heartedly endorsed Hillary Clinton for president of the United States. Holder, the first African American to hold the post of attorney general used his speech to defend the Obama administration's success in fighting violent crime in the United States. After a tumultuous year in which law enforcement officers came under scrutiny over racial injustice in many communities across the country, Holder spoke about these common goals: "safer communities, with less crime, where all our loved ones—police and community residents—come home at night." He used his address to sharply criticize Republican fear-mongering and championed Secretary Clinton's ability to continue to lower crime in the country. Eric Holder Jr. served as the 82nd attorney general of the United States, from 2009 to 2015. Holder is the first African American to hold this position.

I've known Hillary Clinton for almost 25 years—as a friend, a colleague, and a leader of courage and conviction. And today, I am proud to say "I'm with Her!"—because I've seen that she has the skills to serve as commander in chief—and the strength to lead our already-great nation in this hour of challenge and consequence.

At a time when the bonds between law enforcement and communities of color have frayed—when assassins target police in heinous attacks, and peaceful citizens have to question whether black lives truly matter—we need a president who understands the reality I saw, in my travels across the country, as our nation's 82nd Attorney General: that there should be no tension between protecting those who valiantly risk their lives to serve and ensuring that everyone is treated fairly by police.

As the brother of a retired police officer, I am profoundly aware that an attack on a police officer anywhere is an attack on our entire society. So it is not enough for us to praise law enforcement *after* cops are killed. We must protect them, value them—and equip them with the right tools, tactics, and training—while they are still alive. We must also come to realize that keeping our officers safe is not inconsistent with ensuring that those in law enforcement treat the people they are sworn to serve with dignity, respect, and fairness. We must commit ourselves to both goals.

Hillary understands that the goals we share are the same: safer communities, with less crime, where all our loved ones—police and community residents—come

---

Delivered at the Democratic National Convention on July 26, 2016 at the Wells Fargo Center, Philadelphia, Pennsylvania.

home at night. As President, she will continue the work that needs to be done to rebuild trust, because she knows we are Stronger Together.

At a time when our justice system is out of balance, when one in three black men will be incarcerated in their lifetimes, and when black defendants in the federal system receive sentences 20 percent longer than their white peers, we need a president who will end this policy of over-incarceration. As Attorney General, I launched sweeping reforms of our federal criminal justice system and reduced its reliance on draconian mandatory minimum sentences. As a result, we cut the federal prison population and the crime rate—together—for the first time in more than 40 years.

That's right: despite the fiction and fearmongering you've heard from the other party's nominee, violent crime has gone down since President Obama took office.

As President, Hillary will go even further. She fought, as a Senator, against sentencing disparities and racial profiling. She used her first major speech, as a candidate, to lay out a bold vision for criminal justice reform. As a presidential candidate she has talked about systemic racism in a way that no one else has. And she will help our nation summon the courage to confront racial injustice—and face down the legacies of our darkest past.

Finally, at a time when the right to vote is under siege—when Republicans brazenly assault the most fundamental right of our democracy—passing laws designed to stop people from voting, while closing locations in minority neighborhoods where people get the documents they need to vote—we need a president sensitive to these echoes of Jim Crow. We need a president who holds the right to vote as sacred and stands firm against any kind of modern-day poll tax.

My fellow Americans: Hillary Clinton will be that president. She will set a new standard for early voting. She will champion universal, automatic registration—you turn 18, you're registered to vote—because she knows the best way to defend the right to vote is by exercising it.

Throughout history, too many people have sacrificed too much—fought wars, and braved fire hoses, dogs, bullets, and bombs—for this generation to sit on the sidelines.

Never forget that we are heirs to the revolution that began just five miles from where we gather this week and that the choice we face in this pivotal election is about much more than politics.

It's about the arc we are on, as a nation; the composition of our character, as a people; and the ideals—of equality, opportunity, and justice—that have always made America great.

These are the ideals for which Hillary Clinton has fought her entire life. This is the fight she will continue—when we make history by electing her the 45th President of the United States.

Print Citations

CMS: Holder, Eric. "Former Attorney General Addresses the 2016 Democratic National Convention." Speech presented at the Wells Fargo Center, Philadelphia, PA, July, 2016. In *The Reference Shelf: Representative American Speeches 2015-2016*, edited by Betsy Maury, 47-48. Ipswich, MA: H.W. Wilson, 2016.

MLA: Holder, Eric. "Former Attorney General Addresses the 2016 Democratic National Convention." Wells Fargo Center. Philadelphia, PA. July, 2016. Presentation. *The Reference Shelf: Representative American Speeches 2015-2016*. Ed. Betsy Maury. Ipswich: H.W. Wilson, 2016. 47-48. Print.

APA: Holder, E. (2016). Former attorney general Eric Holder addresses the 2016 democratic national convention. [Presentation]. *Speech presented at the Wells Fargo Center*. Philadelphia, PA. In Betsy Maury (Ed.), *The reference shelf: Representative American speeches 2015-2016* (pp. 47-48). Ipswich, MA: H.W. Wilson. (Original work published 2016)

Address by the Speaker of the House at the Republican National Convention

By Paul Ryan

In this speech Representative Paul Ryan endorses the Republican party ticket of Donald Trump and Mike Pence while trying to call for party unity after a fractious primary season that saw Trump, the outsider, draw more support than any other Republican candidate. Here, without specifically outlining Trump's qualifications or track record, Ryan reminds voters of the core Republican party value of limited government and blames the progressive policies of Democrats for many of the country's ills. Paul Ryan is the 54th and current Speaker of the US House of Representatives. Ryan is a member of the Republican Party who has served as the US representative for Wisconsin's 1st congressional district since 1999. He was the Republican Party nominee for vice president of the United States, running alongside former Governor Mitt Romney of Massachusetts in the 2012 election. Ryan is the first person from Wisconsin to hold the position of Speaker of the House.

Delegates, friends, fellow citizens. I can't tell you how much I appreciate the privilege of addressing this 41st convention of the party of Lincoln. And as part of my chairman duties, let me thank all of the people of this beautiful city for looking after us this week. And above all, above all, I want to thank the men and women who are here from law enforcement for your service. You know, standing up here again, it all has kind of a familiar feel. Students of trivia will recall that last time around I was your nominee for vice president. It was a great honor. It was a great honor even if things didn't work out quite according to the plan. Hey, I'm a positive guy. I found some other things to keep me busy. And I like to look at it this way—the next time that there's a State of the Union address, I don't know where Joe Biden or Barack Obama are going to be, but you'll find me right there on the rostrum with Vice President Mike Pence and President Donald Trump.

Democracy is a series of choices. We Republicans have made our choice. Have we had our arguments this year? Sure we have. You know what I call those? Signs of life. Signs of a party that's not just going through the motions, not just mouthing new words for the same old stuff. Meanwhile, what choice has the other party made in this incredible year filled with so many surprises? Here we are, at a time when men and women in both parties so clearly, so undeniably want a big change in direction for America, a clean break from a failed system. And what does the Democratic

Delivered at the Republican National Convention on July 19, 2016, at the Quicken Loans Arena in Cleveland, Ohio.

Party establishment offer? What is their idea of a clean break? They are offering a third Obama term brought to you by another Clinton, and you're supposed to be excited about that.

For a country so ready for change, it feels like we've been cleared for takeoff and then somebody announced that we're all going back to the gate. It's like we've been on hold forever, waiting and waiting to finally talk to a real person and somehow we've been sent back to the main menu. Watch the Democratic Party convention next week, that four-day infomercial of politically correct moralizing, and let it be a reminder of all that is at stake in this election. You could get through four days of it with a little help from the mute button, but four more years of it? Not a chance. Not a chance. Look, the Obama years are almost over. The Clinton years are way over. 2016 is the year America moves on.

From now to November, we will hear how many different ways progressive elitists can find to talk down to the rest of America, to tell the voters that the Obama years have been good for you, that you should be grateful and well now it's Hillary's turn. The problem is really simple. The problem here is very simple. There is a reason people in our country are disappointed and restless. If opportunity seems like it's been slipping away, that's because it has, and liberal progressive ideas have done exactly nothing to help. Wages never seem to go up. The whole economy feels stuck and for millions of Americans, millions of Americans, middle-class security is now just a memory.

Progressives like our president like to talk forever about poverty in America, and if high-sounding talk did any good, we'd have overcome those deep problems long ago. This explains why, under the most liberal president we have had so far, poverty in America is worse, especially for our fellow citizens who are promised better and who need it most. The result is a record of discarded promises, empty gestures, phony strawman arguments, reforms put off forever, shady power-plays like the one that gave us Obamacare, constitutional limits brushed off as nothing, and all the while, dangers in the world downplayed, even as the threats go bolder and come closer.

It's the last chapter of an old story. Progressives deliver everything—except progress. Yet we know better than most. We know better than to think that Republicans can win only on the failures of Democrats. It still comes down to a contest of ideas, which is really good news, ladies and gentlemen, because when it's about ideas the advantage goes to us. Against their dreary backdrop of arrogant bureaucracies, pointless mandates, reckless borrowing, willful retreat from the world and all that progressives have in store for us, the Republican Party stands as the great enduring alternative party. We believe in making government as Ronald Reagan said—not the distributor of gifts and privilege but once again the protector of our liberties. Let the other party go on making its case for more government control over every aspect of our lives, more taxes to pay, more debt to carry, more rules to follow, more judges who make it up as they go along. We in this party—we are committed to a federal government that acts again as a servant, accountable to the people, following the Constitution and venturing not one inch beyond the consent of the governed. We in this party offer a better way for our country, based on fundamentals that go back to the founding generation. We believe in a free society, where aspiration and effort can make the difference in every life. Where your starting point is not your destiny and where your first chance is not your only chance.

We offer a better way for America, with ideas that actually work. A reformed tax code that rewards free enterprise, instead of just enterprising lobbyists. A reformed healthcare system that operates by free choice instead of by force and doesn't leave you answering to cold, clueless bureaucrats. A renewed commitment to building a 21st century military and giving our veterans the care that they were promised and the care that they earned. And we offer a better way for dealing with persistent poverty in this country, a way that shows poor Americans the world beyond liberal warehousing and check-writing, into the life everyone can find with opportunity and independence. The happiness of using your gifts and the dignity of having a job, and you know what, none of this will happen under Hillary Clinton. Only with Donald Trump and Mike Pence do we have a chance at a better way.

And last, last point. Let the other party go on and on with its constant dividing up of people. Always playing one group against the other as if group identity were everything. In America, aren't we all supposed to be and see beyond class, see beyond ethnicity or all these other lines drawn that set us apart and lock us into groups? Real social progress is always a widening of the circle of concern and protection. It's respect and empathy over taking blindness and indifference. It's understanding that by the true measure we are all neighbors and countrymen, a call to each one of us to know what is kind and just and to go and do likewise. Everyone, everyone is equal. Everyone has a place. No one is written off. Because there's worth and goodness in every life. Straight from the Declaration of Independence, that is the Republican ideal, and if we won't defend it, who will?

So much, so much that you and I care about, so many things that we stand for are in the balance in this coming election. Whatever we lack going into this campaign, we should not lack for motivation. In the plainest terms I know, it is all on the line, so let's act that way. Let's act that way. Let's use the edge we have because it is still what earns the trust and the votes. This year of surprises and dramatic terms can end in the finest possible way. When America elects a conservative governing majority, we can do this, we can earn that mandate if we don't hold anything back, if we never lose sight of the stakes, if we never lose sight of what's on the table. Our candidates will be giving their all, they'll be giving their utmost, and every one of us has got to go and do the same.

So what do you say? What do you say? What do you say that we unify this party? What do you say that we unify this party at this crucial moment when unity is everything? Let's take our fight to our opponents with better ideas. Let's get on the offensive and let's stay there. Let's compete in every part of America and turn out to the polls like every last vote matters because it will. Fellow Republicans, what we have begun here, let's see this thing through. Let's win this thing. Let's show America our best and nothing less. Thank you, thank you and God bless.

Print Citations

CMS: Ryan, Paul. "Address by the Speaker of the House at the Republican National Convention." Speech presented at the Quicken Loans Arena, Cleveland, OH, July, 2016. In *The Reference Shelf: Representative American Speeches 2015-2016*, edited by Betsy Maury, 49-51. Ipswich, MA: H.W. Wilson, 2016.

MLA: Ryan, Paul. "Address by the Speaker of the House at the Republican National Convention." Quicken Loans Arena. Cleveland, OH. July, 2016. Presentation. *The Reference Shelf: Representative American Speeches 2015-2016*. Ed. Betsy Maury. Ipswich: H.W. Wilson, 2016. 49-51. Print.

APA: Ryan, P. (2016). Address by the speaker of the house Paul Ryan at the republic national convention. [Presentation]. *Speech presented at the Quicken Loans Arena*. Cleveland, OH. In Betsy Maury (Ed.), *The reference shelf: Representative American speeches 2015-2016* (pp. 49-51). Ipswich, MA: H.W. Wilson. (Original work published 2016)

Remarks on Building a New American Future

By Donald Trump

Hailed by the Washington Post *as candidate Donald Trump's best campaign speech, this address to supporters in Charlotte, NC in the wake of devastating flooding in Louisiana, reveals a compassionate and accessible leader. While the speech contains no specific policy positions, Trump uses the opportunity to talk generally about unity and progress for all Americans by working together and providing opportunities to all people. This platform and promise—to make the nation great again—defined Donald Trump's candidacy for president in 2016. Donald Trump is a billionaire real estate developer and businessman who has starred in his own reality television show. After winning a majority of the primaries and caucuses, Trump became the official Republican candidate for president on July 19, 2016.*

Thank you. It's great to be here in Charlotte. I just met with our many amazing employees right up the road at our property.

I'd like to take a moment to talk about the heartbreak and devastation in Louisiana, a state that is very special to me.

We are one nation. When one state hurts, we all hurt—and we must all work together to lift each other up. Working, building, restoring together.

Our prayers are with the families who have lost loved ones, and we send them our deepest condolences. Though words cannot express the sadness one feels at times like this, I hope everyone in Louisiana knows that our country is praying for them and standing with them to help them in these difficult hours.

We are one country, one people, and we will have together one great future.

Tonight, I'd like to talk about the New American Future we are going to create together.

Last week, I laid out my plan to bring jobs back to our country.

On Monday, I laid out my plan to defeat Radical Islamic Terrorism.

On Tuesday, in Wisconsin, I talked about how we are going to restore law and order to this country.

Delivered at a Trump rally on August 18, 2016, in Charlotte, North Carolina.

Let me take this opportunity to extend our thanks and our gratitude to the police and law enforcement officers in this country who have sacrificed so greatly in these difficult times.

The chaos and violence on our streets, and the assaults on law enforcement, are an attack against all peaceful citizens. If I am elected President, this chaos and violence will end—and it will end very quickly.

Every single citizen in our land has a right to live in safety.

To be one united nation, we must protect all of our people. But we must also provide opportunities for all of our people.

We cannot "Make America Great Again" if we leave any community behind.

Nearly four in ten African-American children are living in poverty. I will not rest until children of every color in this country are fully included in the American Dream.

Jobs, safety, opportunity. Fair and equal representation. This is what I promise to African-Americans, Hispanic-Americans, and all Americans.

But to achieve this New American Future we must break from the failures of the past.

As you know, I am not a politician. I have worked in business, creating jobs and rebuilding neighborhoods my entire adult life. I've never wanted to use the language of the insiders, and I've never been politically correct—it takes far too much time, and can often make it more difficult.

Sometimes, in the heat of debate and speaking on a multitude of issues, you don't choose the right words or you say the wrong thing. I have done that, and I regret it, particularly where it may have caused personal pain. Too much is at stake for us to be consumed with these issues.

But one thing I can promise you is this: I will always tell you the truth.

I speak the truth for all of you, and for everyone in this country who doesn't have a voice.

I speak the truth on behalf of the factory worker who lost his or her job.

I speak the truth on behalf of the veteran who has been denied the medical care they need—and so many are not making it. They are dying.

I speak the truth on behalf of the family living near the border that deserves to be safe in their own country but is instead living with no security at all.

Our campaign is about representing the great majority of Americans—Republicans, Democrats, Independents, Conservatives and Liberals—who read the newspaper, or turn on the TV, and don't hear anyone speaking for them. All they hear are insiders fighting for insiders.

These are the forgotten men and women in our society, and they are angry at so much on so many levels. The poverty, the unemployment, the failing schools, the jobs moving to other countries.

I am fighting for these forgotten Americans.

Fourteen months ago, I declared my campaign for the Presidency on the promise to give our government back to the people. Every day since then, I've worked to repay the loyalty and the faith that you have put in me.

Every day I think about how much is at stake for this country. This isn't just the fight of *my* life, it's the fight of *our* lives—together—to save our country.

I refuse to let another generation of American children be excluded from the American Dream. Our whole country loses when young people of limitless potential are denied the opportunity to contribute their talents because we failed to provide them the opportunities they deserved. Let our children be dreamers too.

Our whole country loses every time a kid doesn't graduate from high school, or fails to enter the workforce or, worse still, is lost to the dreadful world of drugs and crime.

When I look at the failing schools, the terrible trade deals, and the infrastructure crumbling in our inner cities, I know all of this can be fixed - and it can be fixed very quickly.

In the world I come from, if something is broken, you fix it.

If something isn't working, you replace it.

If a product doesn't deliver, you make a change.

I have no patience for injustice, no tolerance for government incompetence, no sympathy for leaders who fail their citizens.

That's why I am running: to end the decades of bitter failure and to offer the American people a new future of honesty, justice and opportunity. A future where America, and its people, always—and I mean always—come first.

Aren't you tired of a system that gets rich at your expense?

Aren't you tired of the same old lies and the same old broken promises? And Hillary Clinton has proven to be one of the greatest liars of all time.

Aren't you tired of arrogant leaders who look down on you, instead of serving and protecting you?

That is all about to change—and it's about to change soon. We are going to put the American people first again.

I've travelled all across this country laying out my bold and modern agenda for change.

In this journey, I will never lie to you. I will never tell you something I do not believe. I will never put anyone's interests ahead of yours.

And, I will never, ever stop fighting for you.

I have no special interest. I am spending millions of dollars on my own campaign—nobody else is.

My only interest is the American people.

So while sometimes I can be too honest, Hillary Clinton is the exact opposite: she never tells the truth. One lie after another, and getting worse each passing day.

The American people are still waiting for Hillary Clinton to apologize for all of the many lies she's told to them, and the many times she's betrayed them.

Tell me, has Hillary Clinton ever apologized for lying about her illegal email server and deleting 33,000 emails?

Has Hillary Clinton apologized for turning the State Department into a pay-for-play operation where favors are sold to the highest bidder?

Has she apologized for lying to the families who lost loved ones at Benghazi?

Has she apologized for putting Iran on the path to nuclear weapons?

Has she apologized for Iraq? For Libya? For Syria? Has she apologized for unleashing ISIS across the world?

Has Hillary Clinton apologized for the decisions she made that have led to so much death, destruction and terrorism?

Speaking of lies, we now know from the State Department announcement that President Obama lied about the $400 million dollars in cash that was flown to Iran. He denied it was for the hostages, but it was. He said we don't pay ransom, but he did. He lied about the hostages—openly and blatantly—just like he lied about Obamacare.

Now the Administration has put every American travelling overseas, including our military personnel, at greater risk of being kidnapped. Hillary Clinton owns President Obama's Iran policy, one more reason she can never be allowed to be President.

Let's talk about the economy. Here, in this beautiful state, so many people have suffered because of NAFTA. Bill Clinton signed the deal, and Hillary Clinton supported it. North Carolina has lost nearly half of its manufacturing jobs since NAFTA went into effect.

Bill Clinton also put China into the World Trade Organization—another Hillary Clinton-backed deal. Your city of Charlotte has lost 1 in 4 manufacturing jobs since China joined the WTO, and many of these jobs were lost while Hillary Clinton was Secretary of State—our chief diplomat with China. She was a disaster, totally unfit for the job.

Hillary Clinton owes the State of North Carolina a very big apology, and I think you'll get that apology around the same time you'll get to see her 33,000 deleted emails.

Another major issue in this campaign has been the border. Our open border has allowed drugs and crime and gangs to pour into our communities. So much needless suffering, so much preventable death. I've spent time with the families of wonderful Americans whose loved ones were killed by the open borders and Sanctuary Cities that Hillary Clinton supports.

I've embraced the crying parents who've lost their children to violence spilling across our border. Parents like Laura Wilkerson and Michelle Root and Sabine Durden and Jamiel Shaw whose children were killed by illegal immigrants.

My opponent supports Sanctuary Cities.

But where was the Sanctuary for Kate Steinle? Where was the Sanctuary for the children of Laura, Michelle, Sabine and Jamiel?

Where was the Sanctuary for every other parent who has suffered so horribly?

These moms and dads don't get a lot of consideration from our politicians. They certainly don't get apologies. They'll never even get the time of day from Hillary Clinton.

But they will always come first to me.

Listen closely: we will deliver justice for all of these American Families. We will create a system of immigration that makes us all proud.

Hillary Clinton's mistakes destroy innocent lives, sacrifice national security, and betray the working families of this country.

Please remember this: I will never put personal profit before national security. I will never leave our border open to appease donors and special interests. I will never support a trade deal that kills American jobs. I will never put the special interests before the national interest. I will never put a donor before a voter, or a lobbyist before a citizen.

Instead, I will be a champion for the people.

The establishment media doesn't cover what really matters in this country, or what's really going on in people's lives. They will take words of mine out of context and spend a week obsessing over every single syllable, and then pretend to discover some hidden meaning in what I said.

Just imagine for a second if the media spent this energy holding the politicians accountable who got innocent Americans like Kate Steinle killed—she was gunned down by an illegal immigrant who had been deported five times.

Just imagine if the media spent time and lots of time investigating the poverty and joblessness of the inner cities. Just think about how much different things would be if the media in this country sent their cameras to our border, to our closing factories, or to our failing schools.

Or if the media focused on what dark streets must be hidden in the 33,000 emails that Hillary Clinton illegally deleted.

Thank you. Instead every story is told from the perspective of the insider. It's the narrative of the people who rig the system, never the voice of the people it's been rigged against. Believe me. So many people suffering for so long in silence. No cameras. No coverage, no outrage from the media class that seems to get outrage over just about everything else. So, again, it's not about me. It's never been about me. It's been about all the people in this country who don't have a voice. I am running to be your voice.

Thank you. I'm running to be the voice for every forgotten part of this country that has been waiting and hoping for a better future.

I am glad that I make the powerful, and I mean very powerful a little uncomfortable now and again, including some of the powerful people, frankly, in my own party because it means that I'm fighting for real change, real change. There is a reason hedge fund managers, the financial lobbyists, the Wall Street investors are throwing their money all over Hillary Clinton because they know she will make sure the system stays rigged in their favor.

It's the powerful protecting the powerful. The insiders fighting for the insiders. I am fighting for you.

Here is the change I propose. On terrorism, we are going to end the era of nation-building and, instead, focus on destroying, destroying, destroying ISIS and radical Islamic terrorism.

We will use military, cyber, and financial warfare and work with any partner in the world and the Middle East that shares our goal in defeating terrorism. I have a message for the terrorists trying to kill our citizens. We will find you, we will destroy you and we will absolutely win and we will win soon.

On immigration, we will temporarily suspend immigration from any place where adequate screening cannot be performed, extreme vetting. Remember, extreme vetting. All applicants for immigration will be vetted for ties to radical ideology. And we will screen out anyone who doesn't share our values and love our people.

Anyone who believes Sharia Law supplants American law will not be given an immigrant visa.

If you want to join our society, then you must embrace our society. Our values, and our tolerant way of life. Those who believe in oppressing women, gays, Hispanics, African-Americans, and people of different faiths are not welcome to join our great country.

We will promote our American values, our American way of life, and our American system of government, which are all, all the best in the world. My opponent on the other hand wants a 550 percent increase in Syrian refugees even more than already pouring into our country under President Obama. Her plan would bring in roughly 620,000 refugees from all refugee-sending nations in her first term alone on top of all other immigration. Think of that. Think of that. What are we doing?

Hillary Clinton is running to be America's Angela Merkel and we have seen how much crime and how many problems that's caused the German people and Germany.

We have enough problems already, we do not need more. On crime we're going to add more police, more investigators, and appoint the best judges and prosecutors in the world.

We will pursue strong enforcement of federal laws. The gangs and cartels. And criminal syndicates terrorizing our people will be stripped apart one by one and they will be sent out of our country quickly. Their day is over. And it's going to end very, very fast. Our trade—thank you. On trade, we're going to renegotiate NAFTA to make it better and if they don't agree, we will withdraw.

And likewise we are going to withdraw from Trans-pacific Partnership, another disaster.

Stand up to China on our terrible trade agreements and protect every last American job. Hillary Clinton has supported all of the major trade deals that have stripped this country of its jobs and its wealth. We owe $20 trillion. On taxes, we are going to massively cut tax rates for workers and small businesses creating millions of new good-paying jobs.

We're going to get rid of regulations that send jobs overseas and we are going to make it easier for young Americans to get the credit they need to start a small business and pursue their dream.

On education, so important, we are going to give students choice and allow charter schools to thrive. We are going to end tenure policies that reward bad teachers and hurt our great, good teachers. My opponent wants to deny student choice and opportunity, all to get a little bit more money from the education bureaucracy. She doesn't care how many young dreams are dashed or destroyed and they are destroyed. Young people are destroyed before they even start. We are going to work closely with African-American parents and children. We are going to work with the parents' students. We are going to work with everybody in the African-American community, in the inner cities, and what a big difference that is going to make. It's one of the things I most look forward to doing.

This means a lot to me and it's going to be a top priority in a Trump administration. On healthcare, we are going to repeal and replace the disaster called ObamaCare. Countless Americans have been forced into part-time jobs, premiums are about to jump by double digits yet again and just this week, AETNA announced it is pulling out of the exchanges all over but also in North Carolina. We are going to replace this disaster with reforms that give you choice and freedom and control in healthcare at a much, much lower cost. You will have much better healthcare at a much lower cost and it will happen quickly.

On political corruption, we are going to restore honor to our government. In my administration, I'm going to enforce all laws concerning the protection of classified information. No one will be above the law. I am going to forbid senior officials from trading favors for cash by preventing them from collecting lavish speaking fees through their spouses when they serve.

I'm going to ask my senior officials to sign an agreement not to accept speaking fees from corporations with a registered lobbyist for five years after leaving office, or from any entity tied to a foreign government.

Finally, we are going to bring our country together. It is so divided. We are going to bring it together. We are going to do it by emphasizing what we all have in common as Americans. We're going to reject bigotry and I will tell you the bigotry of Hillary Clinton is amazing. She sees communities of color only as votes and not as human beings. Worthy of a better future. It's only votes. It is only votes that she sees. And she does nothing about it. She has been there forever and look at where you are. If African-Americans voters give Donald Trump a chance by giving me their vote, the result for them will be amazing.

Look how badly things are going under decades of Democratic leadership. Look at the schools. Look at the poverty. Look at the 58 percent of young African Americans not working. Fifty-eight percent. It is time for a change. What do you have to lose by trying something new? I will fix it watch, I will fix it. We have nothing to lose. Nothing to lose. It is so bad. The inner cities are so bad, you have nothing to lose. They have been playing with you for 60, 70, 80 years, many, many decades. You have nothing to lose. I will do a great job.

This means so much to me. And I will work as hard as I can to bring new opportunity to places in our country which have not known it in a very, very long time. Hillary Clinton and the Democratic Party have taken African-American votes totally for granted. Because the votes have been automatically there for them, there has been no reason for Democrats to produce, and they haven't. They haven't produced in decades and decades. It's time to break with the failures of the past and to fight for every last American child in this country to have a better and a much, much brighter future.

In my administration every American will be treated equally, protected equally and honored equally. We will reject bigotry and hatred and oppression in all of its forms and seek a new future built on our common culture and values as one American people.

This is the change I am promising to all of you, an honest government, a great economy, and a just society for each and every American.

But we can never ever fix our problems by relying on the same politicians who created these problems in the first place. Can't do it. Seventy-two percent of voters say our country is on the wrong track. I am the change candidate. Hillary Clinton is for the failed status quo to protect her special interests, her donors, her lobbyists, and others. It is time to vote for a new American future. Together, we will make America strong again. We will make America proud again, we will make America safe again. Friends and fellow citizens, come November, we will make America great again.

Greater than ever before. Thank you, thank you. And God bless you. Thank you. Thank you. Thank you very much.

Print Citations

CMS: Trump, Donald. "Remarks on Building a New American Future." Speech presented at a Trump rally, Charlotte, NC, August, 2016. In *The Reference Shelf: Representative American Speeches 2015-2016*, edited by Betsy Maury, 54-62. Ipswich, MA: H.W. Wilson, 2016.

MLA: Trump, Donald. "Remarks on Building a New American Future." Trump rally. Charlotte, NC. August, 2016. Presentation. *The Reference Shelf: Representative American Speeches 2015-2016*. Ed. Betsy Maury. Ipswich: H.W. Wilson, 2016. 54-62. Print.

APA: Trump, D. (2016). Remarks on building a new American future. [Presentation]. *Speech presented at a Trump rally*. Charlotte, NC. In Betsy Maury (Ed.), *The reference shelf: Representative American speeches 2015-2016* (pp. 54-62). Ipswich, MA: H.W. Wilson. (Original work published 2016)

Speech at the Democratic Convention

By Cory Booker

In this speech at the Democratic National Convention in Philadelphia, Senator Cory Booker endorses Hillary Clinton for president of the United States. Booker tells voters our nation isn't perfect but that every generation has labored to make our union more perfect. Booker, a rising senator was considered a vice presidential hopeful on the Clinton ticket prior to the naming of Tim Kaine as the Democratic running mate. Here, Booker urges voters to uphold their sacred honor to one another not to simply tolerate Americans of differing opinions but to love them. He strikes a chord of the Clinton campaign message, that we are stronger together. Cory Booker is the junior United States senator from New Jersey, in office since 2013. Previously, he served as mayor of Newark from 2006 to 2013.

Hello, Philadelphia. Thank you. Thank you.

(Applause)

Thank you. Thank you. Thank you. Thank you. Thank you very much. Thank you. Thank you. Thank you very much.

Two hundred and forty years ago, our forefathers gathered in this very city and they declared before the world that we would be a free and independent nation. Today, we gather here again in this city, in this city of brotherly love, to reaffirm our values before our nation and the whole world.

Our purpose is not like theirs, to start a great nation, but to ensure that we continue in the best of our traditions, and with humble homage to generations of patriots before, we put forth two great Americans, our nominees for president and vice president, Hillary Clinton and Tim Kaine.

(Applause)

Now, looking back to our history, looking back to our history, our founding fathers put forth founding documents that were indeed genius. But our founding documents weren't genius because they were perfect. They were saddled with the imperfections and even the bigotry of the past. Native Americans were referred to as savages. Black Americans were fractions of human beings. And women were not mentioned at all.

But those facts and ugly parts of our history don't distract from our nation's greatness.

Delivered at the Democratic National Convention on July 25, 2016, at the Wells Fargo Center, Philadelphia, Pennsylvania.

In fact, I believe we are an even greater nation, not because we started perfect, but because every generation has successfully labored to make us a more perfect union.

(Applause)

Generations of heroic Americans have made our nation more inclusive, more expansive, and more just.

Our nation wasn't founded because we all look alike or prayed alike or descended from the same family tree. But our founders, in their genius, in this, the oldest constitutional democracy on the planet Earth, they put forth the idea that all are created equal, that we have inalienable rights.

And I'm so proud that upon this faithful foundation that we built a great nation. And today, no matter who you are—rich or poor, Asian or white, man or woman, gay or straight, any religion or none at all—you are entitled to the full rights and responsibilities of citizenship.

(Applause)

In this city, our founders put forth a Declaration of Independence, but let me tell you, they also made a historic declaration of interdependence. They knew that if this country was to survive and thrive, we had to make an unusual and extraordinary commitment to each other.

Look, I respect and value the ideals of individualism and self-reliance. But rugged individualism didn't defeat the British. It didn't get us to the moon. It didn't build our nation's highways. Rugged individualism didn't map the human genome. We did that together.

(Applause)

And so this is the high call of patriotism. Patriotism is love of country. But you can't love your country without loving your countrymen and your countrywomen. Now, we don't always have to agree, but we must be there for each other, we must empower each other, we must find the common ground, and we must build bridges across our differences to pursue the common good.

Let me tell you, we cannot devolve into our—to a nation where our highest aspirations are that we just tolerate each other. We are not called to be a nation of tolerance. We are called to be a nation of love.

(Applause)

That's why that last line in the Declaration of Independence says it so clearly. It says that we must—to make this nation work, we must mutually pledge to each other our lives and our fortunes and our sacred honor. Tolerance is the wrong way. Tolerance says I'm just going to stomach your right to be different, that if you disappear from the face of the Earth, I'm no better or worse off.

But love—love knows that every American has worth and value, that no matter what their background, no matter what their race or religion or sexual orientation, love,

love recognizes that we need each other, that we as a nation are better together, that when we are divided we are weak, we decline, yet when we are united, we are strong, when we are indivisible, we are invincible.

(Applause)

This is the understanding of love that's embodied in one of my favorite savings. It's an African saying, and it says, "If you want to go fast, go alone, but if you want to go far, go together."

(Applause)

This is the reason why I am so motivated in this election, because I believe this election is a referendum on who best embodies the leadership we need to go far together.

Donald Trump is not that leader. We've watched him try to get laughs at other people's expense, try to incite fear at a time we need to inspire courage, try to rise in the polls by dragging our national conversation into the gutter. We've watched him mock, cruelly mock a journalist's disability. We've watched him demean the service of my Senate colleague, saying, "He's not a war hero. He was a war hero because he was captured." Trump said, "I don't like people who get captured." Would he say that to POWs from World War II? Would he say that to POWs from Vietnam? Would he say that to the brave men and women in Iraq and Afghanistan right now, risking capture or worse? That's not the commander-in-chief.

We've watched Donald Trump paint with a broad, divisive brush, saying that Mexican immigrants who came to build a better life in America are, in his words, "bringing crime, they're bringing drugs." He called many of them rapists. He said that an Indiana-born federal judge can't be trusted to do his job because of his Mexican ancestry, a statement that his fellow Republicans have described as racist.

(AUDIENCE BOOS)

We've watched Donald Trump, our children, our daughters, our nieces and grandkids have watched Donald Trump and heard him calling women degrading and demeaning names, "Dog." "Fat pig." "Disgusting." "Animal." It's a twisted hypocrisy when he treats other women in a manner he would never, ever accept from another man speaking about his daughters or his wife.

In this great nation, where our founders put a fundamental principle forward of religious freedom, he says ban all Muslims, don't let certain people into our America because of how they pray.

Now, I take particular interest in the fact that Trump says he would run our country like he's run his businesses. Well, I'm from Jersey.

(Applause)

And I'm from the great Garden State. And we've seen how he leads in Atlantic City. He got rich while his companies declared multiple bankruptcies. Yet, without remorse, even as people got hurt and lost jobs by his failures, he bragged, and I quote, "The money I took out of there was incredible."

Yes, he took out a lot of cash, but he stiffed contractors, many of them small businesses, refusing to pay them for the work that they'd done. You know, we in America have seen enough of a handful of people growing rich at the cost of a nation descending into crisis.

(Applause)

America, at our best, we stand up to bullies, and we fight those who seek to demean and degrade other Americans. In times of crisis, we don't abandon our values; we double down on them.

(Applause)

Even amidst the crisis of the Civil War, Lincoln stood up and called out to all of our country, saying, "With malice towards none and charity towards all." This is our history. This is the history that I was taught.

My parents never wanted my brother and I to get too heady. Gratitude was our gravity. So they never stopped reminding me my brother and I that our blessings sprang from countless ordinary Americans who showed extraordinary acts of kindness, decency and love, people who struggled and sweat and bled for our rights, people who paid the ultimate price for the freedoms we all enjoy. I was told that we can't pay those Americans back for their colossal acts of service, but we have an obligation to pay it forward to others through our service and our sacrifice.

(Applause)

I support Hillary Clinton because these are her values, and she has been paying it forward her entire life.

(Applause)

Long before—long before she got in politics, she was in Massachusetts going door-to-door collecting the stories of children with disabilities. In South Carolina, she fought to reform the juvenile justice system so that children wouldn't be thrown in adult prisons. In Alabama, she helped expose the remnants of segregation in schools. In Arkansas, she started a legal aid clinic to make sure poor folks could get their day in court.

She has fought for the people, and she's delivered. That's why we trust her to fight and deliver for us as president.

But let me tell you, we have a presidential nominee in Clinton who knows that, in a time of stunningly wide disparities of wealth in our nation, that America's greatness must not be measured by how many millionaires and billionaires we have, but by how few people we have living in poverty.

Hillary knows that when workers make a fair wage, it doesn't just help their families, it builds a stronger and more durable economy that expands opportunity and makes all of us Americans wealthier.

She knows that in a global knowledge-based economy, the country that out-educates the world will out-earn the world, out-innovate the world, and will lead the world.

She knows that debt-free college is not a gift, it's not charity, it is an investment. It represents the best of our values, the best of our history, and the best of our party, all of our shared ideas and values together.

Hillary Clinton knows that when we have paid family leave that this something that must happen, because when a parent doesn't have to choose between being there for a sick child and paying rent, or when a single mom earns an equal wage for equal work, it empowers the most important building block in all of our nation, and that is the family.

Hillary Clinton knows that security doesn't come from scapegoating other people because of their religion, alienating our allies, stoking fear and pointing fingers. It comes when we band together to face down and defeat our common enemy.

And she knows something that I fight for every day, that our criminal justice system desperately needs reform, that we need to bring back fairness to a system that still, as Professor Bryan Stevenson says, treats you better if you are rich and guilty than poor and innocent.

And she knows that we can be a nation that both believes police officers deserve more respect, they deserve more support, more cooperation and love, and believes that a black 20-something-year-old protestor deserves to be valued, deserves to be held, that they should be listened to with more courageous empathy, and that change is needed in the system.

And Hillary Clinton knows what Donald Trump betrays time and time again in this campaign, that we are not a zero-sum nation. It is not you or me. It is not one American against another American. It is you and I, together, interdependent, interconnected, with one single interwoven destiny.

When we respect each other, when we stand up for each other, when we work together against our challenges, against our neighbors' challenges, be it a neighbor with a beautiful special needs child or one struggling with the ugly disease of addiction, when we as Americans help them, when we show compassion and grace, when we evidence our truth, that we are the United States of America, one nation, under God, indivisible, that is when we are stronger. That is when we go from an already great America to an even greater America.

(Applause)

Now, let me tell you, let me tell you right now, when Trump spews insulting and demeaning words about our fellow Americans, I think of that poem by Maya Angelou.

You all know it. You know how it begins. "You may write me down in history, with your bitter, twisted lies, you may trod me in the very dirt, but still, like dust, I rise."

Well, y'all know it. Y'all know it. This—this—this captures our American history. Two hundred forty years ago, an English king said he would crush our rebellion, but Americans from around our nation joined the fight. From Bunker Hill to the Battle of Trenton, they stood, and so many fell, giving their lives in support of our daring declaration that America, we will rise.

This is our history.

(Applause)

This is our history. Escaped slaves, knowing that liberty is not secure for some until it's secure for all, sometimes hungry, often hunted, in dark woods and deep swamps, they looked up to the North Star and said, with a determined whisper, America, we will rise.

Immigrants, immigrants risking their lives in times of sweatshops and child labor, they organized labor unions and devoted themselves to lifting the tired, the poor, and the huddled masses, with fiercest of grit, they shouted so all could hear, America, we will rise.

King pointed to the mountaintop, Kennedy pointed to the moon, from Seneca Falls to those who stood at Stonewall Inn, giants before us said in a chorus of conviction, America, we will rise.

My fellow Americans—my fellow Americans, we cannot fall into the complacency or indifference about this election, because still the only thing necessary for evil to be triumphant is for good people to do nothing. You know the saying.

My fellow Americans, we cannot be seduced by cynicism about our politics, because cynicism is a refuge for cowards, and this nation is and must always be the home of the brave.

We are the United States of America. We will not falter or fail. We will not retreat or surrender our values. We will not surrender our ideas. We will not surrender the moral high ground.

Here in Philadelphia, let us declare again that we will be a free people. Free from fear and intimidation. Let us declare, again, that we are a nation of interdependence, and that in America, love always trumps hate.

(Applause)

Let us declare—let us declare so that generations yet unborn can hear us. We are the United States of America. Our best days are ahead of us. And together, with Hillary Clinton as our president, America, we will rise.

God bless America. Let us rise together. God bless America.

Print Citations

CMS: Booker, Cory. "Speech at the Democratic National Convention." Speech presented at the Wells Fargo Center, Philadelphia, PA, July, 2016. In *The Reference Shelf: Representative American Speeches 2015-2016*, edited by Betsy Maury, 63-68. Ipswich, MA: H.W. Wilson, 2016.

MLA: Booker, Cory. "Speech at the Democratic National Convention." Wells Fargo Center. Philadelphia, PA. July, 2016. Presentation. *The Reference Shelf: Representative American Speeches 2015-2016*. Ed. Betsy Maury. Ipswich: H.W. Wilson, 2016. 63-68. Print.

APA: Booker, C. (2016). Speech at the democratic national convention. [Presentation]. *Speech presented at the Wells Fargo Center*. Philadelphia, PA. In Betsy Maury (Ed.), *The reference shelf: Representative American speeches 2015-2016* (pp. 63-68). Ipswich, MA: H.W. Wilson. (Original work published 2016)

Address at the Republican National Convention

By Peter Thiel

In one of the shortest speeches of the Republican National Convention in Cleveland, Silicon Valley entrepreneur and businessman Peter Thiel endorsed Donald Trump for president of the United States. Here Thiel turns voters' attention to the country's economic decline in places outside of Silicon Valley, harking back to a time when innovation and prosperity were widely spread out in the United States. In this speech he echoes the message of the Trump campaign—to Make America Great Again—by urging voters not to quarrel over fake culture wars and foreign nation building and focus on a leader who can deliver economic growth. Peter Thiel is a German-American entrepreneur, venture capitalist, and hedge fund manager. He is a well-known Silicon Valley investor who co-founded PayPal and served as its CEO. In 2014 his net worth was valued at $2.2 billion.

Good evening. I'm Peter Thiel. I build companies and I'm supporting people who are building new things, from social networks to rocket ships. I'm not a politician. But neither is Donald Trump. He is a builder, and it's time to rebuild America.

Where I work in Silicon Valley, it's hard to see where America has gone wrong. My industry has made a lot of progress in computers and in software, and, of course, it's made a lot of money. But Silicon Valley is a small place. Drive out to Sacramento, or even just across the bridge to Oakland, and you won't see the same prosperity. That's just how small it is.

Across the country, wages are flat. Americans get paid less today than ten years ago. But healthcare and college tuition cost more every year. Meanwhile Wall Street bankers inflate bubbles in everything from government bonds to Hillary Clinton's speaking fees. Our economy is broken. If you're watching me right now, you understand this better than any politician in Washington DC.

And you know this isn't the dream we looked forward to. Back when my parents came to America looking for that dream, they found it right here in Cleveland. They brought me here as a one-year-old and this is where I became an American. Opportunity was everywhere. My dad studied engineering at Case Western Reserve University, just down the road from where we are now. Because in 1968, the world's high tech capital wasn't just one city: all of America was high tech.

Delivered at the Republican National Convention on July 21, 2016 at the Quicken Loans Arena in Cleveland, Ohio

It's hard to remember this, but our government was once high tech, too. When I moved to Cleveland, defense research was laying the foundations for the Internet. The Apollo program was just about to put a man on the moon–and it was Neil Armstrong, from right here in Ohio. The future felt limitless.

But today our government is broken. Our nuclear bases still use floppy disks. Our newest fighter jets can't even fly in the rain. And it would be kind to say the government's software works poorly, because much of the time it doesn't even work at all. That is a staggering decline for the country that completed the Manhattan Project. We don't accept such incompetence in Silicon Valley, and we must not accept it from our government.

Instead of going to Mars, we have invaded the Middle East. We don't need to see Hillary Clinton's deleted emails: her incompetence is in plain sight. She pushed for a war in Libya, and today it's a training ground for ISIS. On this most important issue Donald Trump is right. It's time to end the era of stupid wars and rebuild our country.

When I was a kid, the great debate was about how to defeat the Soviet Union. And we won. Now we are told that the great debate is about who gets to use which bathroom. This is a distraction from our real problems. Who cares?

Of course, every American has a unique identity. I am proud to be gay. I am proud to be a Republican. But most of all I am proud to be an American. I don't pretend to agree with every plank in our party's platform; but fake culture wars only distract us from our economic decline, and nobody in this race is being honest about it except Donald Trump.

While it is fitting to talk about who we are, today it's even more important to remember where we came from. For me that is Cleveland, and the bright future it promised.

When Donald Trump asks us to Make America Great Again, he's not suggesting a return to the past. He's running to lead us back to that bright future.

Tonight I urge all of my fellow Americans to stand up and vote for Donald Trump.

Print Citations

CMS: Thiel, Peter. "Address at the Republican National Convention." Speech presented at the Quicken Loans Arena, Cleveland, OH, July, 2016. In *The Reference Shelf: Representative American Speeches 2015-2016*, edited by Betsy Maury, 70-71. Ipswich, MA: H.W. Wilson, 2016.

MLA: Thiel, Peter. "Address at the Republican National Convention." Quicken Loans Arena. Cleveland, OH. July, 2016. Presentation. *The Reference Shelf: Representative American Speeches 2015-2016*. Ed. Betsy Maury. Ipswich: H.W. Wilson, 2016. 70-71. Print.

APA: Thiel, P. (2016). Address at the republican national convention. [Presentation]. *Speech presented at the Quicken Loans Arena*. Cleveland, OH. In Betsy Maury (Ed.), *The reference shelf: Representative American speeches 2015-2016* (pp. 70-71). Ipswich, MA: H.W. Wilson. (Original work published 2016)

Super Tuesday Speech

By Bernie Sanders

In this speech in his home state of Vermont, Senator Bernie Sanders thanks his supporters for helping him start his "political revolution" and aims high in continuing his campaign for President of the United States. Considered a long shot in the race for the Democratic nomination beginning with only 3% support in the polls, Sanders ran a robust campaign that promised to transform America. His platform of social and economic justice for ordinary Americans resonated with many voters. Bernie Sanders has served as the junior United States senator from Vermont since 2007. He is the longest-serving independent in US congressional history. In the 2016 Presidential election Sanders raised more money in small, individual contributions than any other candidate in American history in a campaign that was noted for the enthusiasm of millennial voters. After narrowly losing the nomination to Hillary Clinton, Sanders formally endorsed Clinton against her Republican general election opponent Donald Trump, while urging his supporters to continue the "political revolution" his campaign had begun.

SANDERS: Thank you! It is good to be home!

(Applause)

SANDERS: You know, I have been all over this country, but the truth is, it is great and great to come home and see all my friends.

(Applause)

SANDERS: You know, we want to win in every part of the country, that goes without saying. But it does say something and means so much to me that the people who know me best, the people who knew me before I was elected, who knew me as mayor, knew me as congressman, and know me as senator, have voted so strongly to put us in the White House. Thank you so much.

(Applause)

SANDERS: This campaign—as I think all of you know, this campaign is not just about electing the president. It is about transforming America.

(Applause)

SANDERS: It is about making our great country the nation that we know it has the potential to be.

(Applause)

Delivered at Sanders rally on March 1, 2016, in Essex Junction, Vermont.

SANDERS: It is about dealing with some unpleasant truths that exist in America today and having the guts to confront those truths.

(Applause)

SANDERS: It is about recognizing that in our state, we have town meetings and people come out, they argue about budgets, and then they vote. One person, one vote.

(Applause)

SANDERS: In Vermont, billionaires do not buy town meetings, and in America, we are going to end a corrupt campaign finance system.

(Applause)

SANDERS: We can disagree in a democracy, and that's what a democracy is about, but I hope all of us agree that we're going to not allow billionaires and their super PACs to destroy American democracy.

(Applause)

SANDERS: In our state—in our state, you all know that we have many, many thousands of Vermonters who are working not just one job, they're working two jobs, they're working three jobs.

And you all know that while our people are working so hard, almost all of the new wealth and income generated in America is going to the top 1 percent.

Booing.

SANDERS: Well, together, what we are going to do is create an economy that works for all of us, not just the people on top.

(Applause)

SANDERS: And together, we are going to end and reform a broken criminal justice system.

Booing.

SANDERS: This country, the wealthiest country in the history of the world, should not be having more people in jail than any other country on earth. That's wrong.

(Applause)

SANDERS: So we are going to invest for our young people in education, in jobs, not jails or incarceration.

(Applause)

SANDERS: Now, I know many of my Republican colleagues think that climate change is a hoax.

Booing.

SANDERS: Well, I believe that you don't develop real public policy unless you listen to the science, and the science is clear.

(Applause)

SANDERS: Together, we are going to transform our energy system away from fossil fuel to energy efficiency and sustainable energy.

(Applause)

SANDERS: Now, I know that Secretary Clinton and many of the establishment people think that I am looking and thinking too big. I don't think so.

Booing.

SANDERS: So let me go on the record and say as you have heard me say for years, health care is a right for all people.

(Applause)

SANDERS: And let me also say that in the United States of America, when we talk about public education, it's not just first grade through 12th that has got to be expanded to make public colleges and universities tuition-free.

(Applause)

SANDERS: What I have said from day one in this campaign and I suspect many of you were down on the lake with me when we announced on that beautiful day.

(Applause)

SANDERS: What I have said is that this campaign is not just about electing a president. It is about making a political revolution.

(Applause)

SANDERS: What that revolution is about is bringing millions of millions of people into the political process. Working people who have been so disillusioned, they no longer vote. Young people who have never been involved.

What the political revolution is about is bringing our people together. Black and white, Latino, Asian-American.

(Applause)

SANDERS: Gay and straight. People born in America, people who have immigrated to America. When we bring our people together, when we do not allow the Donald Trumps of the world to divide us up.

(Applause)

SANDERS: When we bring our people together and when we have the courage to stand up to the billionaire class and tell them they can't have it all.

(Applause)

SANDERS: That our government belongs to all of us, not just super PACs and wealthy campaign contributors.

(Applause)

SANDERS: Now, tonight, you're going to see a lot of election results come in. And let me remind you of what the media often forgets about. These are not—this is not a general election. It is not winner-take-all. If you get 52 percent, you get 48 percent, you roughly end up with the same amount of delegates in a state. By the end of tonight, we are going to win many hundreds of delegates.

(Applause)

(CHANTS OF "BERNIE")

SANDERS: Ten months ago, as you know better than any other group in America, when we were out on the lake, we were at 3 percent in the polls. We have come a very long way in 10 months.

(Applause)

SANDERS: At the end of tonight, 15 states will have voted, 35 states remain. And let me assure you that we are going to take our fight for economic justice, for social justice, for environmental sanity, for a world of peace to every one of those states.

(Applause)

SANDERS: Now, Wall Street may be against us and the super PACs may be against us. But you know why we're going to win? Because our message is resonating and the people when we stand together will be victorious.

(Applause)

SANDERS: So on a personal note, I want to thank all of you for the love and the friendship that you have given our family. You have sustained me.

(Applause)

SANDERS: And I am so proud to bring Vermont values all across this country.

(Applause)

SANDERS: So thank you again for helping us win here in Vermont tonight.

(Applause)

SANDERS: And I look forward this evening to just saying hello to so many old friends.

So thank you all very much!

(Applause)

Print Citations

CMS: Sanders, Bernie. "Super Tuesday Speech." Speech presented at a Sanders rally, Essex Junction, VT, March, 2016. In *The Reference Shelf: Representative American Speeches 2015-2016*, edited by Betsy Maury, 72-75. Ipswich, MA: H.W. Wilson, 2016.

MLA: Sanders, Bernie. "Super Tuesday Speech." Sanders rally. Essex Junction, VT. March, 2016. Presentation. *The Reference Shelf: Representative American Speeches 2015-2016*. Ed. Betsy Maury. Ipswich: H.W. Wilson, 2016. 72-75. Print.

APA: Sanders, B. (2016). Super Tuesday speech. [Presentation]. *Speech presented at a Sanders rally*. Essex Junction, VT. In Betsy Maury (Ed.), *The reference shelf: Representative American speeches 2015-2016* (pp. 72-75). Ipswich, MA: H.W. Wilson. (Original work published 2016)

America Is Once Again at a Moment of Reckoning

By Hillary Clinton

In this speech on the final night of the Democratic National Convention in Phila-delphia, Hillary Clinton accepts the nomination of her party as candidate for presi-dent of the United States. Her speech highlights both policy positions and speaks to broader voter concerns about economic stagnation and general cynicism. Clinton tells voters about the personal and professional experiences that have prepared her for the job of president. Prior to being the Democratic candidate for President, Hillary Clinton served as secretary of state from 2009 to 2013 and was the junior senator representing New York from 2001 to 2009. Clinton also served as First Lady of the United States during the presidency of her husband Bill Clinton from 1993 to 2001. Clinton became the first female candidate to be nominated for president by a major US political party.

Thank you. Thank you so much. Thank you. Thank you all so much. Thank you. Thank you. Thank you all very, very much. Thank you for that amazing welcome. Thank you all for the great convention that we've had.

And, Chelsea, thank you. I am so proud to be your mother and so proud of the woman you've become. Thank you for bringing Marc into our family and Charlotte and Aidan into the world. And, Bill, that conversation we started in the law library 45 years ago, it is still going strong.

That conversation has lasted through good times that filled us with joy and hard times that tested us. And I've even gotten a few words in along the way. On Tuesday night, I was so happy to see that my explainer-in-chief is still on the job. (Applause.) I'm also grateful to the rest of my family and to the friends of a lifetime.

For all of you whose hard work brought us here tonight and to those of you who joined this campaign this week, thank you. What a remarkable week it's been. We heard the man from Hope, Bill Clinton; and the man of hope, Barack Obama. America is stronger because of President Obama's leadership, and I am better be-cause of his friendship.

We heard from our terrific Vice President, the one and only Joe Biden. He spoke from his big heart about our party's commitment to working people as only he can do.

Delivered on July 29, 2016, at the Democratic National Convention in Philadelphia, Pennsylvania.

And First Lady Michelle Obama reminded us that our children are watching and the president we elect is going to be their president, too.

And for those of you out there who are just getting to know Tim Kaine, you—you will soon understand why the people of Virginia keep promoting him from city council and mayor, to governor, and now Senator. And he will make our whole country proud as our vice president.

And I want to thank Bernie Sanders. Bernie. Bernie, your campaign inspired millions of Americans, particularly the young people who threw their hearts and souls into our primary. You put economic and social justice issues front and center, where they belong.

And to all of your supporters here and around the country, I want you to know I have heard you. Your cause is our cause. Our country needs your ideas, energy, and passion. That is the only way we can turn our progressive platform into real change for America. We wrote it together. Now let's go out and make it happen together.

My friends, we've come to Philadelphia, the birthplace of our nation, because what happened in this city 240 years ago still has something to teach us today. We all know the story, but we usually focus on how it turned out, and not enough on how close that story came to never being written at all. When representatives from 13 unruly colonies met just down the road from here, some wanted to stick with the king, and some wanted to stick it to the king.

The revolution hung in the balance. Then somehow they began listening to each other, compromising, finding common purpose. And by the time they left Philadelphia, they had begun to see themselves as one nation. That's what made it possible to stand up to a king. That took courage. They had courage. Our founders embraced the enduring truth that we are stronger together.

Now America is once again at a moment of reckoning. Powerful forces are threatening to pull us apart. Bonds of trust and respect are fraying. And just as with our founders, there are no guarantees. It truly is up to us. We have to decide whether we will all work together so we can all rise together. Our country's motto is e pluribus unum: out of many, we are one. Will we stay true to that motto?

Well, we heard Donald Trump's answer last week at his convention. He wants to divide us from the rest of the world and from each other. He's betting that the perils of today's world will blind us to its unlimited promise. He's taken the Republican Party a long way from "Morning in America" to "Midnight in America." He wants us to fear the future and fear each other.

Well, a great Democratic President, Franklin Delano Roosevelt, came up with the perfect rebuke to Trump more than eighty years ago, during a much more perilous time: "The only thing we have to fear is fear itself."

Now we are clear-eyed about what our country is up against, but we are not afraid. We will rise to the challenge, just as we always have. We will not build a wall. Instead, we will build an economy where everyone who wants a good job can get one.

And we'll build a path to citizenship for millions of immigrants who are already contributing to our economy. We will not ban a religion. We will work with all Americans and our allies to fight and defeat terrorism.

Yet, we know there is a lot to do. Too many people haven't had a pay raise since the crash. There's too much inequality, too little social mobility, too much paralysis in Washington, too many threats at home and abroad.

But just look for a minute at the strengths we bring as Americans to meet these challenges. We have the most dynamic and diverse people in the world. We have the most tolerant and generous young people we've ever had. We have the most powerful military, the most innovative entrepreneurs, the most enduring values—freedom and equality, justice and opportunity. We should be so proud that those words are associated with us. I have to tell you, as your Secretary of State, I went to 112 countries. When people hear those words, they hear America.

So don't let anyone tell you that our country is weak. We're not. Don't let anyone tell you we don't have what it takes. We do. And most of all, don't believe anyone who says, "I alone can fix it." Yes. Those were actually Donald Trump's words in Cleveland. And they should set off alarm bells for all of us. Really? "I alone can fix it?" Isn't he forgetting troops on the front lines, police officers and firefighters who run toward danger, doctors and nurses who care for us? Teachers who change lives, entrepreneurs who see possibilities in every problem, mothers who lost children to violence and are building a movement to keep other kids safe? He's forgetting every last one of us. Americans don't say, "I alone fix can it." We say, "We'll fix it together."

And remember. Remember. Our founders fought a revolution and wrote a Constitution so America would never be a nation where one person had all the power. 240 years later, we still put our faith in each other. Look at what happened in Dallas. After the assassinations of five brave police officers, Police Chief David Brown asked the community to support his force, maybe even join them. And do you know how the community responded? Nearly 500 people applied in just 12 days.

That's how Americans answer when the call for help goes out. 20 years ago, I wrote a book called *It Takes a Village*. And a lot of people looked at the title and asked, what the heck do you mean by that? This is what I mean. None of us can raise a family, build a business, heal a community, or lift a country totally alone. America needs every one of us to lend our energy, our talents, our ambition to making our nation better and stronger. I believe that with all my heart. That's why "Stronger Together" is not just a lesson from our history, it's not just a slogan for our campaign, it's a guiding principle for the country we've always been, and the future we're going to build.

A country where the economy works for everyone, not just those at the top. Where you can get a good job and send your kids to a good school no matter what zip code you live in. A country where all our children can dream, and those dreams are within reach. Where families are strong, communities are safe, and, yes, where love trumps hate. That's the country we're fighting for. That's the future we're working toward.

And so, my friends, it is with humility, determination, and boundless confidence in America's promise that I accept your nomination for president of the United States.

Now, sometimes the people at this podium are new to the national stage. As you know, I'm not one of those people. I've been your First Lady, served eight years as a senator from the great state of New York. Then I represented all of you as Secretary of State. But my job titles only tell you what I've done. They don't tell you why. The truth is, through all these years of public service, the service part has always come easier to me than the public part. I get it that some people just don't know what to make of me. So let me tell you.

The family I'm from, well, no one had their name on big buildings. My families were builders of a different kind, builders in the way most American families are. They used whatever tools they had, whatever God gave them, and whatever life in America provided, and built better lives and better futures for their kids.

My grandfather worked in the same Scranton lace mill for 50 years because he believed that if he gave everything he had, his children would have a better life than he did. And he was right. My dad, Hugh, made it to college. He played football at Penn State and enlisted in the Navy after Pearl Harbor. When the war was over he started his own small business, printing fabric for draperies. I remember watching him stand for hours over silkscreens. He wanted to give my brothers and me opportunities he never had, and he did.

My mother, Dorothy, was abandoned by her parents as a young girl. She ended up on her own at 14, working as a housemaid. She was saved by the kindness of others. Her first grade teacher saw she had nothing to eat at lunch, and brought extra food to share the entire year. The lesson she passed on to me years later stuck with me: No one gets through life alone. We have to look out for each other and lift each other up. And she made sure I learned the words from our Methodist faith: "Do all the good you can, for all the people you can, in all the ways you can, as long as ever you can."

So I went to work for the Children's Defense Fund, going door to door in New Bedford, Massachusetts on behalf of children with disabilities who were denied the chance to go to school. Remember meeting a young girl in a wheelchair on the small back porch of her house. She told me how badly she wanted to go to school. It just didn't seem possible in those days. And I couldn't stop thinking of my mother and what she'd gone through as a child. It became clear to me that simply caring is not enough. To drive real progress, you have to change both hearts and laws. You need both understanding and action.

So we gathered facts. We build a coalition. And our work helped convince Congress to ensure access to education for all students with disabilities. It's a big idea, isn't it? Every kid with a disability has the right to go to school. But how do you make an idea like that real? You do it step by step, year by year, sometimes even door by door. My heart just swelled when I saw Anastasia Somoza representing millions of young people on this stage because we changed our law to make sure she got an education.

So it's true. I sweat the details of policy, whether we're talking about the exact level of lead in the drinking water in Flint, Michigan the number of mental health facilities in Iowa, or the cost of your prescription drugs. Because it's not just a detail if it's your kid, if it's your family. It's a big deal. And it should be a big deal to your president, too.

After the four days of this convention, you've seen some of the people who've inspired me, people who let me into their lives and became a part of mine, people like Ryan Moore and Lauren Manning. They told their stories Tuesday night. I first met Ryan as a 7-year-old. He was wearing a full body brace that must have weighed 40 pounds because I leaned over to lift him up. Children like Ryan kept me going when our plan for universal health care failed, and kept me working with leaders of both parties to help create the Children's Health Insurance Program that covers eight million kids in our country. Lauren Manning, who stood here with such grace and power, was gravely injured on 9/11.

It was the thought of her, and Debbie Stage. John who you saw in the movie, and John Dolan and Joe Sweeney and all the victims and survivors, that kept me working as hard as I could in the Senate on behalf of 9/11 families and our first responders who got sick from their time at Ground Zero. I was thinking of Lauren, Debbie, and all the others ten years later in the White House Situation Room, when President Obama made the courageous decision that finally brought Osama bin Laden to justice.

And in this campaign I've met many more people who motivate me to keep fighting for change, and with your help, I will carry all of your voices and stories with me to the White House. And you heard from Republicans and Independents who are supporting our campaign. Well, I will be a president for Democrats, Republicans, Independents, for the struggling, the striving, the successful, for all those who vote for me and for those who don't. For all Americans together.

Tonight, we've reached a milestone in our nation's march toward a more perfect union: the first time that a major party has nominated a woman for president. Standing here as my mother's daughter, and my daughter's mother, I'm so happy this day has come. I'm happy for grandmothers and little girls and everyone in between. I'm happy for boys and men—because when any barrier falls in America, it clears the way for everyone. After all, when there are no ceilings, the sky's the limit. So let's keep going until every one of the 161 million women and girls across America has the opportunity she deserves to have. But even more important than the history we make tonight is the history we will write together in the years ahead. Let's begin with what we're going to do to help working people in our country get ahead and stay ahead.

Now, I don't think President Obama and Vice President Biden get the credit they deserve for saving us from the worst economic crisis of our lifetimes. Our economy is so much stronger than when they took office. Nearly 15 million new private sector jobs. Twenty million more Americans with health insurance. And an auto industry that just had its best year ever. Now, that's real progress. But none of us can be satisfied with the status quo. Not by a long shot. We're still facing deep-seated problems that developed long before the recession and have stayed with us through the recovery. I've gone around the country talking to working families. And I've heard from many who feel like the economy sure isn't working for them. Some of you are frustrated—even furious. And you know what? You're right. It's not yet working the way it should.

Americans are willing to work—and work hard. But right now, an awful lot of people feel there is less and less respect for the work they do. And less respect for them, period. Democrats, we are the party of working people. But we haven't done a good enough job showing we get what you're going through, and we're going to do something to help.

So tonight I want to tell you how we will empower Americans to live better lives. My primary mission as president will be to create more opportunity and more good jobs with rising wages right here in the United States. From my first day in office to my last. Especially in places that for too long have been left out and left behind. From our inner cities to our small towns, from Indian country to coal country. From communities ravaged by addiction to regions hollowed out by plant closures.

And here's what I believe. I believe America thrives when the middle class thrives. I believe our economy isn't working the way it should because our democracy isn't working the way it should. That's why we need to appoint Supreme Court justices who will get money out of politics and expand voting rights, not restrict them. And if necessary, we will pass a constitutional amendment to overturn Citizens United.

I believe American corporations that have gotten so much from our country should be just as patriotic in return. Many of them are, but too many aren't. It's wrong to take tax breaks with one hand and give out pink slips with the other. And I believe Wall Street can never, ever be allowed to wreck Main Street again.

And I believe in science. I believe that climate change is real and that we can save our planet while creating millions of good-paying clean energy jobs.

I believe that when we have millions of hardworking immigrants contributing to our economy, it would be self-defeating and inhumane to try to kick them out. Comprehensive immigration reform will grow our economy and keep families together—and it's the right thing to do. So whatever party you belong to, or if you belong to no party at all, if you share these beliefs, this is your campaign.

If you believe that companies should share profits, not pad executive bonuses, join us. If you believe the minimum wage should be a living wage, and no one working full-time should have to raise their children in poverty, join us. If you believe that every man, woman, and child in America has the right to affordable health care, join us! If you believe that we should say no to unfair trade deals; that we should stand up to China; that we should support our steelworkers and autoworkers and homegrown manufacturers, then join us.

If you believe we should expand Social Security and protect a woman's right to make her own heath care decisions, then join us. And yes, yes, if you believe that your working mother, wife, sister, or daughter deserves equal pay join us. That's how we're going to make sure this economy works for everyone, not just those at the top.

Now, you didn't hear any of this, did you, from Donald Trump at his convention. He spoke for 70-odd minutes—and I do mean odd. And he offered zero solutions. But we already know he doesn't believe these things. No wonder he doesn't like talking about his plans. You might have noticed, I love talking about mine.

In my first 100 days, we will work with both parties to pass the biggest investment in new, good-paying jobs since World War II. Jobs in manufacturing, clean energy, technology and innovation, small business, and infrastructure. If we invest in infrastructure now, we'll not only create jobs today, but lay the foundation for the jobs of the future.

And we will also transform the way we prepare our young people for those jobs. Bernie Sanders and I will work together to make college tuition-free for the middle class and debt-free for all. We will also—we will also liberate millions of people who already have student debt. It's just not right that Donald Trump can ignore his debts, and students and families can't refinance their debts.

And something we don't say often enough: Sure, college is crucial, but a four-year degree should not be the only path to a good job. We will help more people learn a skill or practice a trade and make a good living doing it. We will give small businesses, like my dad's, a boost, make it easier to get credit. Way too many dreams die in the parking lots of banks. In America, if you can dream it, you should be able to build it.

And we will help you balance family and work. And you know what, if fighting for affordable child care and paid family leave is playing the "woman card," then deal me in.

Now—now, here's the other thing. Now, we're not only going to make all of these investments. We're going to pay for every single one of them. And here's how. Wall Street, corporations, and the super-rich are going to start paying their fair share of taxes. This is—this is not because we resent success, but when more than 90 percent of the gains have gone to the top 1 percent, that's where the money is. And we are going to follow the money. And if companies take tax breaks and then ship jobs overseas, we'll make them pay us back. And we'll put that money to work where it belongs: creating jobs here at home.

Now, I imagine that some of you are sitting at home thinking, well, that all sounds pretty good, but how are you going to get it done? How are you going to break through the gridlock in Washington? Well, look at my record. I've worked across the aisle to pass laws and treaties and to launch new programs that help millions of people. And if you give me the chance, that's exactly what I'll do as President.

But then—but then I also imagine people are thinking out there, but Trump, he's a businessman. He must know something about the economy. Well, let's take a closer look, shall we? In Atlantic City, 60 miles from here, you will find contractors and small businesses who lost everything because Donald Trump refused to pay his bills. Now, remember what the President said last night. Don't boo. Vote.

But think of this. People who did the work and needed the money, not because he couldn't pay them, but because he wouldn't pay them, he just stiffed them. And you know that sales pitch he's making to be president: put your faith in him, and you'll win big? That's the same sales pitch he made to all those small businesses. Then Trump walked away and left working people holding the bag.

He also talks a big game about putting America first. Well, please explain what part of America First leads him to make Trump ties in China, not Colorado; Trump suits in Mexico, not Michigan; Trump furniture in Turkey, not Ohio; Trump picture frames in India, not Wisconsin. Donald Trump says he wants to make America great again. Well, he could start by actually making things in America again.

Now, the choice we face in this election is just as stark when it comes to our national security.

Anyone—anyone reading the news can see the threats and turbulence we face. From Baghdad and Kabul, to Nice and Paris and Brussels, from San Bernardino to Orlando, we're dealing with determined enemies that must be defeated. So it's no wonder that people are anxious and looking for reassurance, looking for steady leadership, wanting a leader who understands we are stronger when we work with our allies around the world and care for our veterans here at home. Keeping our nation safe and honoring the people who do that work will be my highest priority.

I'm proud that we put a lid on Iran's nuclear program without firing a single shot. Now we have to enforce it, and we must keep supporting Israel's security. I'm proud that we shaped a global climate agreement. Now we have to hold every country accountable to their commitments, including ourselves. And I'm proud to stand by our allies in NATO against any threat they face, including from Russia.

I've laid out my strategy for defeating ISIS. We will strike their sanctuaries from the air and support local forces taking them out on the ground. We will surge our intelligence so we detect and prevent attacks before they happen. We will disrupt their efforts online to reach and radicalize young people in our country. It won't be easy or quick, but make no mistake we will prevail.

Now Donald Trump—Donald Trump says, and this is a quote, "I know more about ISIS than the generals do." No, Donald, you don't.

He thinks—he thinks he knows more than our military because he claimed our armed forces are "a disaster." Well, I've had the privilege to work closely with our troops and our veterans for many years, including as a Senator on the Armed Services Committee. And I know how wrong he is. Our military is a national treasure. We entrust our commander-in-chief to make the hardest decisions our nation faces:

decisions about war and peace, life and death. A president should respect the men and women who risk their lives to serve our country, including—including Captain Khan and the sons of Tim Kaine and Mike Pence, both Marines. So just ask yourself: Do you really think Donald Trump has the temperament to be commander-in-chief? Donald Trump can't even handle the rough-and-tumble of a presidential campaign. He loses his cool at the slightest provocation—when he's gotten a tough question from a reporter, when he's challenged in a debate, when he sees a protestor at a rally. Imagine, if you dare imagine, imagine him in the Oval Office facing a real crisis. A man you can bait with a tweet is not a man we can trust with nuclear weapons.

I can't put it any better than Jackie Kennedy did after the Cuban Missile Crisis. She said that what worried President Kennedy during that very dangerous time was that a war might be started—not by big men with self-control and restraint, but by little men, the ones moved by fear and pride.

America's strength doesn't come from lashing out. It relies on smarts, judgment, cool resolve, and the precise and strategic application of power. And that's the kind of commander-in-chief I pledge to be.

And if we're serious about keeping our country safe, we also can't afford to have a president who's in the pocket of the gun lobby. I'm not here to repeal the Second Amendment. I'm not here to take away your guns. I just don't want you to be shot by someone who shouldn't have a gun in the first place.

We will work tirelessly with responsible gun owners to pass common-sense reforms and keep guns out of the hands of criminals, terrorists, and all others who would do us harm.

For decades, people have said this issue was too hard to solve and the politics too hot to touch. But I ask you: How can we just stand by and do nothing? You heard, you saw, family members of people killed by gun violence on this stage. You heard, you saw family members of police officers killed in the line of duty because they were outgunned by criminals. I refuse to believe we can't find common ground here. We have to heal the divides in our country, not just on guns but on race, immigration, and more.

And that starts with listening, listening to each other, trying as best we can to walk in each other's shoes. So let's put ourselves in the shoes of young black and Latino men and women who face the effects of systemic racism and are made to feel like their lives are disposable. Let's put ourselves in the shoes of police officers, kissing their kids and spouses goodbye every day and heading off to do a dangerous and necessary job. We will reform our criminal justice system from end to end, and rebuild trust between law enforcement and the communities they serve. And we will defend—we will defend all our rights: civil rights, human rights, and voting rights; women's rights and workers' rights; LGBT rights and the rights of people with disabilities. And we will stand up against mean and divisive rhetoric wherever it comes from.

For the past year, many people made the mistake of laughing off Donald Trump's comments, excusing him as an entertainer just putting on a show. They thought he couldn't possibly mean all the horrible things he says, like when he called women "pigs" or said that an American judge couldn't be fair because of his Mexican heritage, or when he mocks and mimics a reporter with a disability, or insults prisoners of war—like John McCain, a hero and a patriot who deserves our respect.

Now, at first, I admit, I couldn't believe he meant it, either. It was just too hard to fathom, that someone who wants to lead our nation could say those things, could be like that. But here's the sad truth: There is no other Donald Trump. This is it. And in the end, it comes down to what Donald Trump doesn't get: America is great because America is good.

So enough with the bigotry and the bombast. Donald Trump's not offering real change. He's offering empty promises. And what are we offering? A bold agenda to improve the lives of people across our country—to keep you safe, to get you good jobs, to give your kids the opportunities they deserve.

The choice is clear, my friends. Every generation of Americans has come together to make our country freer, fairer, and stronger. None of us ever have or can do it alone. I know that at a time when so much seems to be pulling us apart, it can be hard to imagine how we'll ever pull together. But I'm here to tell you tonight—progress is possible. I know. I know because I've seen it in the lives of people across America who get knocked down and get right back up.

And I know it from my own life. More than a few times, I've had to pick myself up and get back in the game. Like so much else in my life, I got this from my mother too. She never let me back down from any challenge. When I tried to hide from a neighborhood bully, she literally blocked the door. "Go back out there," she said. And she was right. You have to stand up to bullies. You have to keep working to make things better, even when the odds are long and the opposition is fierce.

We lost our mother a few years ago, but I miss her every day. And I still hear her voice urging me to keep working, keep fighting for right, no matter what. That's what we need to do together as a nation. And though "we may not live to see the glory," as the song from the musical Hamilton goes, "let us gladly join the fight." Let our legacy be about "planting seeds in a garden you never get to see."

That's why we're here, not just in this hall, but on this Earth. The Founders showed us that, and so have many others since. They were drawn together by love of country, and the selfless passion to build something better for all who follow. That is the story of America. And we begin a new chapter tonight.

Yes, the world is watching what we do. Yes, America's destiny is ours to choose. So let's be stronger together, my fellow Americans. Let's look to the future with courage and confidence. Let's build a better tomorrow for our beloved children and our beloved country. And when we do, America will be greater than ever.

Thank you and may God bless you and the United States of America.

Print Citations

CMS: Clinton, Hillary. "America Is Once Again at a Moment of Reckoning." Speech presented at the Wells Fargo Center, Philadelphia, PA, July, 2016. In *The Reference Shelf: Representative American Speeches 2015-2016*, edited by Betsy Maury, 77-86. Ipswich, MA: H.W. Wilson, 2016.

MLA: Clinton, Hillary. "America Is Once Again at a Moment of Reckoning." Wells Fargo Center. Philadelphia, PA. July, 2016. Presentation. *The Reference Shelf: Representative American Speeches 2015-2016*. Ed. Betsy Maury. Ipswich: H.W. Wilson, 2016. 77-86. Print.

APA: Clinton, H. (2016). America is once again at a moment of reckoning. [Presentation]. *Speech presented at the Wells Fargo Center*. Philadelphia, PA. In Betsy Maury (Ed.), *The reference shelf: Representative American speeches 2015-2016* (pp. 77-86). Ipswich, MA: H.W. Wilson. (Original work published 2016)

Donald Trump's Acceptance Speech

By Donald Trump

A tumultuous and divisive 2016 presidential campaign ended on November 8th when Republican candidate Donald J. Trump emerged victorious as the 45th President-elect of the United States. This short acceptance speech aimed to thank supporters, campaign workers, and Republican backers while promising to bring the country together as one united people. Speaking of his populist movement, Trump thanks the forgotten people of America for placing their trust in him and promises a broad economic renewal plan that taps into the nation's potential for greatness. Donald John Trump is an American businessman and television personality. He is scheduled to take office as the 45th President on January 20, 2017.

Thank you. Thank you very much, everybody. Sorry to keep you waiting. Complicated business. Complicated. Thank you very much.

I've just received a call from Secretary Clinton. She congratulated us. It's about us. On our victory, and I congratulated her and her family on a very, very hard-fought campaign.

I mean, she fought very hard. Hillary has worked very long and very hard over a long period of time, and we owe her a major debt of gratitude for her service to our country.

I mean that very sincerely.

Now it is time for America to bind the wounds of division, have to get together. To all Republicans and Democrats and independents across this nation, I say it is time for us to come together as one united people. It is time. I pledge to every citizen of our land that I will be President for all of Americans, and this is so important to me. For those who have chosen not to support me in the past, of which there were a few people, I'm reaching out to you for your guidance and your help so that we can work together and unify our great country.

As I've said from the beginning, ours was not a campaign but rather an incredible and great movement, made up of millions of hard-working men and women who love their country and want a better, brighter future for themselves and for their family.

Delivered on November 9, 2016, in New York, New York.

It is a movement comprised of Americans from all races, religions, backgrounds, and beliefs, who want and expect our government to serve the people—and serve the people it will.

Working together, we will begin the urgent task of rebuilding our nation and renewing the American dream. I've spent my entire life in business, looking at the untapped potential in projects and in people all over the world. That is now what I want to do for our country. Tremendous potential. I've gotten to know our country so well. Tremendous potential. It is going to be a beautiful thing. Every single American will have the opportunity to realize his or her fullest potential. The forgotten men and women of our country will be forgotten no longer.

We are going to fix our inner cities and rebuild our highways, bridges, tunnels, airports, schools, hospitals. We're going to rebuild our infrastructure, which will become, by the way, second to none. And we will put millions of our people to work as we rebuild it.

We will also finally take care of our great veterans who have been so loyal, and I've gotten to know so many over this 18-month journey. The time I've spent with them during this campaign has been among my greatest honors. Our veterans are incredible people.

We will embark upon a project of national growth and renewal. I will harness the creative talents of our people, and we will call upon the best and brightest to leverage their tremendous talent for the benefit of all. It is going to happen. We have a great economic plan. We will double our growth and have the strongest economy anywhere in the world. At the same time, we will get along with all other nations willing to get along with us. We will be. We will have great relationships. We expect to have great, great relationships.

No dream is too big, no challenge is too great. Nothing we want for our future is beyond our reach. America will no longer settle for anything less than the best. We must reclaim our country's destiny and dream big and bold and daring. We have to do that. We're going to dream of things for our country, and beautiful things and successful things once again.

I want to tell the world community that while we will always put America's interests first, we will deal fairly with everyone, with everyone. All people and all other nations.

We will seek common ground, not hostility; partnership, not conflict.

And now I would like to take this moment to thank some of the people who really helped me with this, what they are calling tonight a very, very historic victory.

First, I want to thank my parents, who I know are looking down on me right now. Great people. I've learned so much from them. They were wonderful in every regard. Truly great parents. I also want to thank my sisters, Marianne and Elizabeth, who are here with us tonight. Where are they? They're here someplace. They're very shy, actually.

And my brother Robert, my great friend. Where is Robert? Where is Robert?

My brother Robert, and they should be on this stage, but that's okay. They're great.

And also my late brother Fred, great guy. Fantastic guy. Fantastic family. I was very lucky. Great brothers, sisters, great, unbelievable parents.

To Melania and Don and Ivanka and Eric and Tiffany and Barron, I love you and I thank you, and especially for putting up with all of those hours. This was tough.

This was tough. This political stuff is nasty, and it is tough. So I want to thank my family very much. Really fantastic. Thank you all. Thank you all.

Lara, unbelievable job. Unbelievable. Vanessa, thank you. Thank you very much. What a great group. You've all given me such incredible support, and I will tell you that we have a large group of people. You know, they kept saying we have a small staff. Not so small. Look at all of the people that we have. Look at all of these people.

And Kellyanne and Chris and Rudy and Steve and David. We have got tremendously talented people up here, and I want to tell you it's been very, very special.

I want to give a very special thanks to our former mayor, Rudy Giuliani. He's unbelievable. Unbelievable. He traveled with us and he went through meetings, and Rudy never changes. Where is Rudy? Where is he? Gov. Chris Christie, folks, was unbelievable. Thank you, Chris. The first man, first senator, first major, major politician. Let me tell you, he is highly respected in Washington because he is as smart as you get.

Sen. Jeff Sessions. Where is Jeff? A great man. Another great man, very tough competitor. He was not easy. He was not easy. Who is that? Is that the mayor that showed up? Is that Rudy?

Up here. Really a friend to me, but I'll tell you, I got to know him as a competitor because he was one of the folks that was negotiating to go against those Democrats, Dr. Ben Carson. Where's Ben? Where is Ben? By the way, Mike Huckabee is here someplace, and he is fantastic. Mike and his family Sarah, thank you very much. Gen. Mike Flynn. Where is Mike? And Gen. Kellogg. We have over 200 generals and admirals that have endorsed our campaign and they are special people.

We have 22 Congressional Medal of Honor people. A very special person who, believe me, I read reports that I wasn't getting along with him. I never had a bad second with him. He's an unbelievable star. He is ... that's right, how did you possibly guess? Let me tell you about Reince. I've said Reince. I know it. I know it. Look at all of those people over there. I know it, Reince is a superstar. I said, they can't call you a superstar, Reince, unless we win it. Like Secretariat. He would not have that bust at the track at Belmont.

Reince is really a star and he is the hardest-working guy, and in a certain way I did this . Reince, come up here. Get over here, Reince.

Boy, oh, boy, oh, boy. It's about time you did this right. My god. Nah, come here. Say something.

Amazing guy. Our partnership with the RNC was so important to the success and what we've done, so I also have to say, I've gotten to know some incredible people.

The Secret Service people. They're tough and they're smart and they're sharp and I don't want to mess around with them, I can tell you. And when I want to go and wave to a big group of people and they rip me down and put me back down in the seat, but they are fantastic people so I want to thank the Secret Service.

And law enforcement in New York City, they're here tonight. These are spectacular people, sometimes underappreciated unfortunately. We appreciate them.

So it's been what they call a historic event, but to be really historic, we have to do a great job, and I promise you that I will not let you down. We will do a great job. We will do a great job. I look very much forward to being your president, and hopefully at the end of two years or three years or four years or maybe even eight years you will say so many of you worked so hard for us, with you. You will say that—you will say that that was something that you were—really were very proud to do and I can — thank you very much.

And I can only say that while the campaign is over, our work on this movement is now really just beginning. We're going to get to work immediately for the American people, and we're going to be doing a job that hopefully you will be so proud of your President. You will be so proud. Again, it's my honor.

It's an amazing evening. It's been an amazing two-year period, and I love this country. Thank you.

Thank you very much. Thank you to Mike Pence.

Print Citations

CMS: Trump, Donald. "Donald Trump's Acceptance Speech." New York, NY, November, 2016. In *The Reference Shelf: Representative American Speeches 2015-2016*, edited by Betsy Maury, 88-91. Ipswich, MA: H.W. Wilson, 2016.

MLA: Trump, Donald. "Donald Trump's Acceptance Speech." New York, NY. November, 2016. Presentation. *The Reference Shelf: Representative American Speeches 2015-2016*. Ed. Betsy Maury. Ipswich: H.W. Wilson, 2016. 88-91. Print.

APA: Trump, D. (2016). Donald Trump's Acceptance Speech. [Presentation]. New York, NY. In Betsy Maury (Ed.), *The reference shelf: Representative American speeches 2015-2016* (pp. 88-91). Ipswich, MA: H.W. Wilson. (Original work published 2016)

3
Civil Rights
and
Social Justice

(L-R) NBA players Carmelo Anthony, Chris Paul, Dwyane Wade and LeBron James speak onstage during the 2016 ESPYS at Microsoft Theater on July 13, 2016 in Los Angeles, California.

Remarks at a Press Conference Announcing a Complaint Against the State of North Carolina to Stop Discrimination Against Transgender Individuals

By Loretta Lynch

In this statement, Attorney General Loretta Lynch apprises the public of the ongoing legislative battle between the state of North Carolina and the federal government over transgender bathroom rights. Here, she announces a federal civil rights lawsuit against the state of North Carolina, Governor Pat McCrory, the North Carolina Department of Public Safety and the University of North Carolina over the passing of House Bill 2, North Carolina's Public Facilities and Security Act, prescribing that transgender people use public bathrooms according to the gender assigned to them at birth. Lynch ties transgender rights to civil rights by citing Brown v. Board of Education *and the* Emancipation Proclamation. *Loretta Lynch is the 83rd and current attorney general of the United States. She was sworn in on April 27, 2015 and is the first African-American woman to be confirmed for the position.*

Good afternoon and thank you all for being here. Today, I'm joined by [Vanita] Gupta, head of the Civil Rights Division at the Department of Justice. We are here to announce a significant law enforcement action regarding North Carolina's Public Facilities Privacy & Security Act, also known as House Bill 2.

The North Carolina General Assembly passed House Bill 2 in special session on March 23 of this year. The bill sought to strike down an anti-discrimination provision in a recently-passed Charlotte, North Carolina, ordinance, as well as to require transgender people in public agencies to use the bathrooms consistent with their sex as noted at birth, rather than the bathrooms that fit their gender identity. The bill was signed into law that same day. In so doing, the legislature and the governor placed North Carolina in direct opposition to federal laws prohibiting discrimination on the basis of sex and gender identity. More to the point, they created state-sponsored discrimination against transgender individuals, who simply seek to engage in the most private of functions in a place of safety and security—a right taken for granted by most of us.

Delivered on May 9, 2016 in Washington, DC

Last week, our Civil Rights Division notified state officials that House Bill 2 violates federal civil rights laws. We asked that they certify by the end of the day today that they would not comply with or implement House Bill 2's restriction on restroom access. An extension was requested by North Carolina and was under active consideration. But instead of replying to our offer or providing a certification, this morning, the state of North Carolina and its governor chose to respond by suing the Department of Justice. As a result of their decisions, we are now moving forward.

Today, we are filing a federal civil rights lawsuit against the state of North Carolina, Governor Pat McCrory, the North Carolina Department of Public Safety and the University of North Carolina. We are seeking a court order declaring House Bill 2's restroom restriction impermissibly discriminatory, as well as a statewide bar on its enforcement. While the lawsuit currently seeks declaratory relief, I want to note that we retain the option of curtailing federal funding to the North Carolina Department of Public Safety and the University of North Carolina as this case proceeds.

This action is about a great deal more than just bathrooms. This is about the dignity and respect we accord our fellow citizens and the laws that we, as a people and as a country, have enacted to protect them—indeed, to protect all of us. And it's about the founding ideals that have led this country—haltingly but inexorably—in the direction of fairness, inclusion and equality for all Americans.

This is not the first time that we have seen discriminatory responses to historic moments of progress for our nation. We saw it in the Jim Crow laws that followed the Emancipation Proclamation. We saw it in fierce and widespread resistance to *Brown v. Board of Education*. And we saw it in the proliferation of state bans on same-sex unions intended to stifle any hope that gay and lesbian Americans might one day be afforded the right to marry. That right, of course, is now recognized as a guarantee embedded in our Constitution, and in the wake of that historic triumph, we have seen bill after bill in state after state taking aim at the LGBT community. Some of these responses reflect a recognizably human fear of the unknown, and a discomfort with the uncertainty of change. But this is not a time to act out of fear. This is a time to summon our national virtues of inclusivity, diversity, compassion and open-mindedness. What we must not do—what we must never do—is turn on our neighbors, our family members, our fellow Americans, for something they cannot control, and deny what makes them human. This is why none of us can stand by when a state enters the business of legislating identity and insists that a person pretend to be something they are not, or invents a problem that doesn't exist as a pretext for discrimination and harassment.

Let me speak now to the people of the great state, the beautiful state, my state of North Carolina. You've been told that this law protects vulnerable populations from harm—but that just is not the case. Instead, what this law does is inflict further indignity on a population that has already suffered far more than its fair share. This law provides no benefit to society—all it does is harm innocent Americans.

Instead of turning away from our neighbors, our friends, our colleagues, let us instead learn from our history and avoid repeating the mistakes of our past. Let us reflect on the obvious but often neglected lesson that state-sanctioned discrimination never looks good in hindsight. It was not so very long ago that states, including North Carolina, had signs above restrooms, water fountains and on public accommodations keeping people out based upon a distinction without a difference. We have moved beyond those dark days, but not without pain and suffering and an ongoing fight to keep moving forward. Let us write a different story this time. Let us not act out of fear and misunderstanding, but out of the values of inclusion, diversity and regard for all that make our country great.

Let me also speak directly to the transgender community itself. Some of you have lived freely for decades. Others of you are still wondering how you can possibly live the lives you were born to lead. But no matter how isolated or scared you may feel today, the Department of Justice and the entire Obama Administration wants you to know that we see you; we stand with you; and we will do everything we can to protect you going forward. Please know that history is on your side. This country was founded on a promise of equal rights for all, and we have always managed to move closer to that promise, little by little, one day at a time. It may not be easy—but we'll get there together.

I want to thank my colleagues in the Civil Rights Division who have devoted many hours to this case so far, and who will devote many more to seeing it through. At this time, I'd like to turn things over to Vanita Gupta, whose determined leadership on this and so many other issues has been essential to the Justice Department's work.

Print Citations

CMS: Lynch, Loretta. "Remarks at a Press Conference Announcing a Complaint Against the State of North Carolina to Stop Discrimination Against Transgender Individuals." Washington, DC, May, 2016. In *The Reference Shelf: Representative American Speeches 2015-2016*, edited by Betsy Maury, 95-97. Ipswich, MA: H.W. Wilson, 2016.

MLA: Lynch, Loretta. "Remarks at a Press Conference Announcing a Complaint Against the State of North Carolina to Stop Discrimination Against Transgender Individuals." Washington, DC. May, 2016. Presentation. *The Reference Shelf: Representative American Speeches 2015-2016*. Ed. Betsy Maury. Ipswich: H.W. Wilson, 2016. 95-97. Print.

APA: Lynch, L. (2016). Remarks at a press conference announcing a complaint against the state of North Carolina to stop discrimination against transgender individuals. [Presentation]. Washington, DC. In Betsy Maury (Ed.), *The reference shelf: Representative American speeches 2015-2016* (pp. 95-97). Ipswich, MA: H.W. Wilson. (Original work published 2016)

Race at the BET Awards

By Jesse Williams

In this speech, actor and activist Jesse Williams takes the opportunity to remind the audience and TV viewers of the widespread racial injustice in America. He urges African Americans to take part in the necessary struggle for equal rights and criticizes the white community for appropriating black creative genius. Jesse Williams is an American actor, model, and activist, best known for his role as Dr. Jackson Avery on the ABC Television series Grey's Anatomy. *In 2016, Williams was executive producer of the documentary film* Stay Woke: The Black Lives Matter Movement. *He won the Black Entertainment Television (BET) humanitarian award in 2016.*

Peace peace. Thank you, Debra. Thank you, BET. Thank you Nate Parker, Harry and Debbie Allen for participating in that.

Before we get into it, I just want to say I brought my parents out tonight. I just want to thank them for being here, for teaching me to focus on comprehension over career, and that they make sure I learn what the schools were afraid to teach us. And also thank my amazing wife for changing my life.

Now, this award—this is not for me. This is for the real organizers all over the country—the activists, the civil rights attorneys, the struggling parents, the families, the teachers, the students that are realizing that a system built to divide and impoverish and destroy us cannot stand if we do.

It's kind of basic mathematics—the more we learn about who we are and how we got here, the more we will mobilize.

Now, this is also in particular for the black women in particular who have spent their lifetimes dedicated to nurturing everyone before themselves. We can and will do better for you.

Now, what we've been doing is looking at the data and we know that police somehow manage to deescalate, disarm and not kill white people everyday. So what's going to happen is we are going to have equal rights and justice in our own country or we will restructure their function and ours.

Now… I got more y'all—yesterday would have been young Tamir Rice's 14th birthday so I don't want to hear anymore about how far we've come when paid public servants can pull a drive-by on 12 year old playing alone in the park in broad daylight,

Delivered on June 27, 2016, at the Black Entertainment Awards in Los Angeles, California.

killing him on television and then going home to make a sandwich. Tell Rekia Boyd how it's so much better than it is to live in 2012 than it is to live in 1612 or 1712. Tell that to Eric Garner. Tell that to Sandra Bland. Tell that to Dorian Hunt.

Now the thing is, though, all of us in here getting money—that alone isn't gonna stop this. Alright, now dedicating our lives, dedicating our lives to getting money just to give it right back for someone's brand on our body when we spent centuries praying with brands on our bodies, and now we pray to get paid for brands on our bodies.

There has been no war that we have not fought and died on the front lines of. There has been no job we haven't done. There is no tax they haven't levied against us—and we've paid all of them. But freedom is somehow always conditional here. "You're free," they keep telling us. But she would have been alive if she hadn't acted so… free.

Now, freedom is always coming in the hereafter, but you know what, though, the hereafter is a hustle. We want it now.

And let's get a couple things straight, just a little side note—the burden of the brutalized is not to comfort the bystander. That's not our job, alright—stop with all that. If you have a critique for the resistance, for our resistance, then you better have an established record of critique of our oppression. If you have no interest, if you have no interest in equal rights for black people then do not make suggestions to those who do. Sit down.

We've been floating this country on credit for centuries, yo, and we're done watching and waiting while this invention called whiteness uses and abuses us, burying black people out of sight and out of mind while extracting our culture, our dollars, our entertainment like oil—black gold, ghettoizing and demeaning our creations then stealing them, gentrifying our genius and then trying us on like costumes before discarding our bodies like rinds of strange fruit. The thing is though… the thing is that just because we're magic doesn't mean we're not real.

Thank you.

Print Citations

CMS: Williams, Jesse. "Race at the BET Awards." Speech presented at the Black Entertainment Awards, Los Angeles, CA, June, 2016. In *The Reference Shelf: Representative American Speeches 2015-2016*, edited by Betsy Maury, 98-99. Ipswich, MA: H.W. Wilson, 2016.

MLA: Williams, Jesse. "Race at the BET Awards." Black Entertainment Awards. Los Angeles, CA. June, 2016. Presentation. *The Reference Shelf: Representative American Speeches 2015-2016*. Ed. Betsy Maury. Ipswich: H.W. Wilson, 2016. 98-99. Print.

APA: Williams, J. (2016). Race at the BET awards. [Presentation]. *Speech presented at the Black Entertainment Awards*. Los Angeles, CA. In Betsy Maury (Ed.), *The reference shelf: Representative American speeches 2015-2016* (pp. 98-99). Ipswich, MA: H.W. Wilson. (Original work published 2016)

Why We Need Gender-Neutral Bathrooms

By Ivan Coyote

In this popular TEDx talk in Vancouver in November 2015, transgender storyteller and author Ivan Coyote discusses the basic need for gender-neutral bathrooms in public places. They appeal to a sense of common humanity for any living person with privacy issues in public places. Ivan Coyote is the Canadian award-winning author of eleven books, the creator of four short films, and has released three albums that combine storytelling with music. Ivan is a transgender individual who speaks on issues of gender identity in their work, as well as topics such as family, class, social justice, and queer liberation.

There are a few things that all of us need. We all need air to breathe. We need clean water to drink. We need food to eat. We need shelter and love. You know. Love is great, too. And we all need a safe place to pee.

(Laughter) Yeah?

As a trans person who doesn't fit neatly into the gender binary, if I could change the world tomorrow to make it easier for me to navigate, the very first thing I would do is blink and create single stall, gender-neutral bathrooms in all public places.

(Applause) Trans people and trans issues, they've been getting a lot of mainstream media attention lately. And this is a great and necessary thing, but most of that attention has been focused on a very few individuals, most of whom are kinda rich and pretty famous, and probably don't have to worry that much anymore about where they're going to pee in between classes at their community college, or where they're going to get changed into their gym strip at their public high school. Fame and money insulates these television star trans people from most of the everyday challenges that the rest of us have to tackle on a daily basis.

Public bathrooms. They've been a problem for me since as far back as I can remember, first when I was just a little baby tomboy and then later as a masculine-appearing, predominantly estrogen-based organism.

(Laughter)

Now, today as a trans person, public bathrooms and change rooms are where I am most likely to be questioned or harassed. I've often been verbally attacked behind their doors. I've been hauled out by security guards with my pants still halfway

Delivered at TEDx in Vancouver, Canada in November 2015.

pulled up. I've been stared at, screamed at, whispered about, and one time I got smacked in the face by a little old lady's purse that from the looks of the shiner I took home that day I am pretty certain contained at least 70 dollars of rolled up small change and a large hard candy collection.

(Laughter)

And I know what some of you are thinking, and you're mostly right. I can and do just use the men's room most of the time these days. But that doesn't solve my change room dilemmas, does it? And I shouldn't have to use the men's room because I'm not a man. I'm a trans person.

And now we've got these fear-mongering politicians that keep trying to pass these bathroom bills. Have you heard about these? They try to legislate to try and force people like myself to use the bathroom that they deem most appropriate according to the gender I was assigned at birth. And if these politicians ever get their way, in Arizona or California or Florida or just last week in Houston, Texas, or Ottawa, well then, using the men's room will not be a legal option for me either.

And every time one of these politicians brings one of these bills to the table, I can't help but wonder, you know, just who will and exactly how would we go about enforcing laws like these. Right? Panty checks? Really. Genital inspections outside of bath change rooms at public pools? There's no legal or ethical or plausible way to enforce laws like these anyway. They exist only to foster fear and promote transphobia. They don't make anyone safer. But they do for sure make the world more dangerous for some of us.

And meanwhile, our trans children suffer. They drop out of school, or they opt out of life altogether. Trans people, especially trans and gender-nonconforming youth face additional challenges when accessing pools and gyms, but also universities, hospitals, libraries. Don't even get me started on how they treat us in airports.

If we don't move now to make sure that these places are truly open and accessible to everyone, then we just need to get honest and quit calling them public places. We need to just admit that they are really only open for people who fit neatly into one of two gender boxes, which I do not. I never have. And this starts very early.

I know a little girl. She's the daughter of a friend of mine. She's a self-identified tomboy. I'm talking about cowboy boots and Caterpillar yellow toy trucks and bug jars, the whole nine yards. One time I asked her what her favorite color was. She told me, "Camouflage."

(Laughter)

So that awesome little kid, she came home from school last October from her half day of preschool with soggy pants on because the other kids at school were harassing her when she tried to use the girls' bathroom. And the teacher had already instructed her to stay out of the boys' bathroom. And she had drank two glasses of that red juice at the Halloween party, and I mean, who can resist that red juice, right? It's so good. And she couldn't hold her pee any longer.

Her and her classmates were four years old. They already felt empowered enough to police her use of the so-called public bathrooms. She was four years old. She had already been taught the brutal lesson that there was no bathroom door at preschool with a sign on it that welcomed people like her. She'd already learned that bathrooms were going to be a problem, and that problem started with her and was hers alone. So my friend asked me to talk to her little daughter, and I did. I wanted to tell her that me and her mom were going to march on down and talk to that school, and the problem was going to go away, but I knew that wasn't true. I wanted to tell her that it was all going to get better when she got older, but I couldn't. So I asked her to tell me the story of what had happened, asked her to tell me how it made her feel. "Mad and sad," she told me. So I told her that she wasn't alone and that it wasn't right what had happened to her, and then she asked me if I had ever peed in my pants before. I said yes, I had, but not for a really long time.

(Laughter)

Which of course was a lie, because you know how you hit, like, 42 or 43, and sometimes you just, I don't know, you pee a little bit when you cough or sneeze, when you're running upstairs, or you're stretching. Don't lie. It happens. Right? She doesn't need to know that, I figure.

(Laughter)

I told her, when you get older, your bladder is going to grow bigger, too. When you get old like me, you're going to be able to hold your pee for way longer, I promised her.

"Until you can get home?" she asked me.

I said, "Yes, until you can get home." She seemed to take some comfort in that.

So let's just build some single stall, gender-neutral bathrooms with a little bench for getting changed into your gym clothes. We can't change the world overnight for our children, but we can give them a safe and private place to escape that world, if only for just a minute. This we can do. So let's just do it.

And if you are one of those people who is sitting out there right now already coming up with a list of reasons in your head why this is not a priority, or it's too expensive, or telling yourself that giving a trans person a safe place to pee or get changed in supports a lifestyle choice that you feel offends your morality, or your masculinity, or your religious beliefs, then let me just appeal to the part of your heart that probably, hopefully, does care about the rest of the population. If you can't bring yourself to care enough about people like me, then what about women and girls with body image issues? What about anyone with body image stuff going on? What about that boy at school who is a foot shorter than his classmates, whose voice still hasn't dropped yet? Hey? Oh, grade eight, what a cruel master you can be. Right? What about people with anxiety issues? What about people with disabilities or who need assistance in there? What about folks with bodies who, for whatever reason, don't fit into the mainstream idea of what a body should look like? How many of us still feel shy or afraid to disrobe in front of our peers, and how many of us allow that fear to keep us from something as important as physical exercise? Would all those people not benefit from these single stall facilities?

We can't change transphobic minds overnight, but we can give everybody a place to get changed in so that we can all get to work making the world safer for all of us.

Thank you for listening.

(Applause)

Thank you.

(Applause)

Print Citations

CMS: Coyote, Ivan. "Why We Need Gender-Neutral Bathrooms." Speech presented at Tedx Talk, Vancouver, Canada, November, 2015. In *The Reference Shelf: Representative American Speeches 2015-2016*, edited by Betsy Maury, 101-104. Ipswich, MA: H.W. Wilson, 2016.

MLA: Coyote, Ivan. "Why We Need Gender-Neutral Bathrooms." Tedx Talk. Vancouver, Canada. November, 2015. Presentation. *The Reference Shelf: Representative American Speeches 2015-2016*. Ed. Betsy Maury. Ipswich: H.W. Wilson, 2016. 101-104. Print.

APA: Coyote, I. (2016). Why we need gender-neutral bathrooms. [Presentation]. *Speech presented at Tedx Talk*. Vancouver, Canada. In Betsy Maury (Ed.), *The reference shelf: Representative American speeches 2015-2016* (pp. 101-104). Ipswich, MA: H.W. Wilson. (Original work published 2016)

The Law Enforcement Profession and Historical Injustices

By Terrence M. Cunningham

In this speech delivered at the annual gathering of the International Association of Chiefs of Police in 2016, Chief Cunningham not only recognizes the historic role that the police have played mistreating fellow citizens in communities of color, he apologizes for past wrongs. While acknowledging this injustice he calls for both police officers and communities of color to put this historic mistrust behind them in order to build a mutually safe future together. Chief Terrence M. Cunningham has over 30 years of experience as a police officer, and is chief of police in Wellesley, Massachusetts. He is currently the president of the International Association of Chiefs of Police (IACP).

I would like to take a moment to address a significant and fundamental issue confronting our profession, particularly within the United States. Clearly, this is a challenging time for policing. Events over the past several years have caused many to question the actions of our officers and has tragically undermined the trust that the public must and should have in their police departments. At times such as this, it is our role as leaders to assess the situation and take the steps necessary to move forward.

This morning, I would like to address one issue that I believe will help both our profession and our communities. The history of the law enforcement profession is replete with examples of bravery, self-sacrifice, and service to the community. At its core, policing is a noble profession made up of women and men who have sworn to place themselves between the innocent and those who seek to do them harm.

Over the years, thousands of police officers have laid down their lives for their fellow citizens while hundreds of thousands more have been injured while protecting their communities. The nation owes all of those officers, as well as those who are still on patrol today, an enormous debt of gratitude.

At the same time, it is also clear that the history of policing has also had darker periods.

There have been times when law enforcement officers, because of the laws enacted by federal, state, and local governments, have been the face of oppression for far too many of our fellow citizens. In the past, the laws adopted by our society have required police officers to perform many unpalatable tasks, such as ensuring legalized

Remarks delivered on October 17, 2016 at the IACP Annual Conference and Exposition in San Diego, California.

discrimination or even denying the basic rights of citizenship to many of our fellow Americans.

While this is no longer the case, this dark side of our shared history has created a multigenerational—almost inherited—mistrust between many communities of color and their law enforcement agencies.

Many officers who do not share this common heritage often struggle to comprehend the reasons behind this historic mistrust. As a result, they are often unable to bridge this gap and connect with some segments of their communities.

While we obviously cannot change the past, it is clear that we must change the future. We must move forward together to build a shared understanding. We must forge a path that allows us to move beyond our history and identify common solutions to better protect our communities.

For our part, the first step in this process is for law enforcement and the IACP to acknowledge and apologize for the actions of the past and the role that our profession has played in society's historical mistreatment of communities of color.

At the same time, those who denounce the police must also acknowledge that today's officers are not to blame for the injustices of the past. If either side in this debate fails to acknowledge these fundamental truths, we will be unlikely to move past them.

Overcoming this historic mistrust requires that we must move forward together in an atmosphere of mutual respect. All members of our society must realize that we have a mutual obligation to work together to ensure fairness, dignity, security, and justice.

It is my hope that, by working together, we can break this historic cycle of mistrust and build a better and safer future for us all.

Print Citations

CMS: Cunningham, Terrence M. "The Law Enforcement Profession and Historical Injustice." Speech presented at the IACP Annual Conference and Exposition, San Diego, CA, October, 2016. In *The Reference Shelf: Representative American Speeches 2015-2016*, edited by Betsy Maury, 105-106. Ipswich, MA: H.W. Wilson, 2016.

MLA: Cunningham, Terrence M. "The Law Enforcement Profession and Historical Injustice." IACP Annual Conference and Exposition. San Diego, CA. October, 2016. Presentation. *The Reference Shelf: Representative American Speeches 2015-2016*. Ed. Betsy Maury. Ipswich: H.W. Wilson, 2016. 105-106. Print.

APA: Cunningham, T. M. (2016). The law enforcement profession and historical injustice. [Presentation]. *Speech presented at the IACP Annual Conference and Exposition*. San Diego, CA. In Betsy Maury (Ed.), *The reference shelf: Representative American speeches 2015-2016* (pp. 105-106). Ipswich, MA: H.W. Wilson. (Original work published 2016)

Gun Violence and Racial Turmoil

By LeBron James, Carmelo Anthony, Chris Paul and Dwyane Wade

This speech, by four leading African American athletes, was delivered as part of the opening ceremony of the 2016 ESPY Awards. The athletes, in their own words, call for greater leadership among athletes and celebrities in building safe communities, setting positive examples and standing up against violence. All of the athletes are professional basketball players in the NBA.

Carmelo Anthony

Good evening. Tonight is a celebration of sports, celebrating our accomplishments and our victories. But, in this moment of celebration, we asked to start the show tonight this way, the four of us talking to our fellow athletes, with the country watching.

Because we cannot ignore the reality of the current state of America. The events of the past week have put a spotlight on the injustice, distrust and anger that plague so many of us.

The system is broken. The problems are not new. The violence is not new. And the racial divide definitely is not new.

But the urgency to create change is at an all-time high.

Chris Paul

We stand here tonight accepting our role in uniting communities, to be the change we need to see. We stand before you as fathers, sons, husbands, brothers, uncles and in my case, as an African-American man and the nephew of a police officer, who is one of the hundreds of thousands of great officers serving this country.

But, Trayvon Martin. Michael Brown. Tamir Rice. Eric Garner. Laquan McDonald. Alton Sterling. Philando Castile.

This is also our reality.

Generations ago, legends like Jesse Owens, Jackie Robinson, Muhammad Ali, John Carlos and Tommie Smith, Kareem Abdul-Jabbar, Jim Brown, Billie

Delivered at the ESPY Awards at the Microsoft Theater on Wednesday, July 13, 2016, in Los Angeles, California.

Jean King, Arthur Ashe and countless others, they set a model for what athletes should stand for.

So we choose to follow in their footsteps.

Dwyane Wade

The racial profiling has to stop. The shoot-to-kill mentality has to stop. Not seeing the value of black and brown bodies has to stop. But also, the retaliation has to stop.

The endless gun violence in places like Chicago, Dallas, not to mention Orlando, it has to stop. Enough. Enough is enough.

Now, as athletes, it's on us to challenge each other to do even more than we already do in our own communities. And the conversation, it cannot stop as our schedules get busy again. It won't always be convenient. It won't. It won't always be comfortable, but it is necessary.

LeBron James

We all feel helpless and frustrated by the violence. We do. But that's not acceptable. It's time to look in the mirror and ask ourselves what are we doing to create change.

It's not about being a role model. It's not about our responsibility to a tradition of activism.

I know tonight we're honoring Muhammad Ali. The GOAT. But to do his legacy any justice, let's use this moment as a call to action for all professional athletes to educate ourselves. It's for these issues. Speak up. Use our influence. And renounce all violence.

And most importantly, go back to our communities, invest our time, our resources, help rebuild them, help strengthen them, help change them.

We all have to do better. Thank you.

Print Citations

CMS: James, LeBron, Anthony, Carmelo, Paul, Chris, and Dwyane Wade. "Gun Violence and Racial Turmoil." Speech presented at the ESPY Awards, Los Angeles, CA, July, 2016. In *The Reference Shelf: Representative American Speeches 2015-2016*, edited by Betsy Maury, 108-109. Ipswich, MA: H.W. Wilson, 2016.

MLA: James, LeBron, et al. "Gun Violence and Racial Turmoil." ESPY Awards. Los Angeles, CA. July, 2016. Presentation. *The Reference Shelf: Representative American Speeches 2015-2016*. Ed. Betsy Maury. Ipswich: H.W. Wilson, 2016. 108-09. Print.

APA: James, L., Anthony, C., Paul, C., & Wade, D. (2016). Gun violence and racial turmoil. [Presentation]. *Speech presented at the ESPY Awards*. Los Angeles, CA. In Betsy Maury (Ed.), *The reference shelf: Representative American speeches 2015-2016* (pp. 108-109). Ipswich, MA: H.W. Wilson. (Original work published 2016)

Statement on Legislation That Protects the Privacy of North Carolina Citizens

By Pat McCrory

This speech, delivered over video by North Carolina Governor Pat McCrory attempts to defend the signing of House Bill 2. House Bill 2 eliminates nondiscrimination ordinances and effectively legalizes discrimination against LGBT people in North Carolina. More specifically, it forces transgender students in public schools and workers in government buildings to use bathrooms and other facilities that are strictly consistent with their gender identity on birth documents, not with the gender identity they claim. This speech was delivered as the bill was passed and signed into law. North Carolina's bathroom laws gained national attention in 2016 as courts considered LGBT civil rights. Pat McCrory is the Republican governor of North Carolina. He previously served as mayor of the city of Charlotte.

Hi, I'm North Carolina Governor Pat McCrory.

In the 50 plus years since I've lived in North Carolina I've learned that the people of North Carolina love each other and they respect their differences. Even when those differences conflict with their beliefs and values.

Time and time again I've witnessed the people of North Carolina put aside their disagreements and come together to accommodate and work out solutions, while still respecting each other's beliefs and values.

I've also witnessed politicians who have exploited differences and divided our people. Instead of living up to the North Carolina tradition of respecting those with whom they disagree they've demonized our state for political gain. And that is not acceptable.

Some have called our state an embarrassment. The real embarrassment is politicians not publicly respecting each other's positions on complex issues.

Unfortunately, that has occurred when legislation was passed to protect men, women and children when they use a public restroom, shower or locker-room. That is an expectation of privacy that must be honored and respected.

Instead, North Carolina has been the target of a vicious, nation-wide smear campaign. Disregarding the facts, other politicians, from the White House to mayors and city council members and yes our Attorney General, have initiated and promoted

Delivered as a televised video speech on March 29, 2016 in Raleigh, N.C.

conflict to advance their political agenda. Even if it means defying the constitution and their oath of office.

Obeying the laws of the land, living up to the duties of the office and defending the constitution is the foundation of my governorship. I am standing up to the president of the United States to prevent federal overreach to take over our North Carolina waters in violation of the U.S. Constitution.

I even stood up to the legislative leaders of my own party when they took powers not delegated to them in the North Carolina constitution, and our Supreme Court agreed.

Now I'm standing up to the Attorney General of North Carolina who today refused to fulfill his oath of office to defend the people of North Carolina in a lawsuit filed over the privacy of our restrooms. As the state's attorney, he can't select which laws he will defend and which laws are politically expedient to refuse to defend.

His excuse that his own internal policies would be affected is wrong. All employment policies for cities and corporations and the Attorney General's own policies remain the same. The Attorney General is inventing conflict that simply doesn't exist.

When you are the state's lawyer, you are a lawyer first and a politician second. Therefore, I encourage the Attorney General to reconsider his flawed logic. I am fulfilling my oath of office as governor of North Carolina and we expect him to do the same as attorney general.

As elected officials we don't get to choose the perfect circumstances that surround the decisions we have to make under the constitution.

I did not call for a special session. I expressed concerns over some of the provisions that were in the legislation. But at the end of the day the General Assembly acted within the provisions of the constitution and presented me with a bill that, while it may not be perfect, provided protection of our basic expectation of privacy in public restrooms and locker rooms.

I signed that bill because if I didn't, on April 1st, the expectation of privacy of North Carolina citizens could be violated.

This is not about demonizing one group of people. Let's put aside our differences, the political rhetoric and yes, hypocrisy, and work on solutions that will make this bill better in the future. I am open to new ideas and solutions.

And to the people and businesses of North Carolina: we are a state of inclusiveness, openness and diversity.

I believe in North Carolina, its people and our democratic process. And I will not shy away from taking the responsibility to do what it takes to make our state better.

Those were the values I learned more than 50 years ago when I first came to North Carolina and I will continue to uphold those values as your governor.

May God Bless you and the people of North Carolina.

Print Citations

CMS: McCrory, Pat. "Statement on Legislation That Protects the Privacy of North Carolina Citizens." Speech presented in Raleigh, North Carolina, March, 2016. In *The Reference Shelf: Representative American Speeches 2015-2016*, edited by Betsy Maury, 111-13. Ipswich, MA: H.W. Wilson, 2016.

MLA: McCrory, Pat. "Statement on Legislation That Protects the Privacy of North Carolina Citizens." Raleigh, NC. March, 2016. Presentation. *The Reference Shelf: Representative American Speeches 2015-2016*. Ed. Betsy Maury. Ipswich: H.W. Wilson, 2016. 111-13. Print.

APA: McCrory, P. (2016). Statement on legislation that protects the privacy of North Carolina citizens. [Presentation]. Raleigh, NC. In Betsy Maury (Ed.), *The reference shelf: Representative American speeches 2015-2016* (pp. 111-113). Ipswich, MA: H.W. Wilson. (Original work published 2016)

4
The Year in Review

Keith Bedford/The Boston Globe via Getty Images

US First Lady Michelle Obama speaks during a campaign rally in support of U.S. Democratic Presidential nominee Hillary Clinton at Southern New Hampshire University in Manchester, NH on Oct. 13, 2016.

Statement on the Clinton
E-mail Investigation

By James Comey

In these remarks director of the FBI, James Comey, reports on the status of the investigation into then Secretary of State Hillary Clinton's e-mails sent and received on her private server. Comey outlines the nature of the e-mails, the degrees of classification and the reconstructing of over 30,000 e-mail threads turned over by Secretary Clinton during her time at the State Department. While Comey calls Secretary Clinton's handling of classified information "extremely careless" his investigation did not find her in violation of the laws governing handling of classified information. In this speech, the FBI recommends to the Justice Department that no charges be brought against Secretary Clinton. James Comey Jr. is the current director of the Federal Bureau of Investigation.

Good morning. I'm here to give you an update on the FBI's investigation of Secretary Clinton's use of a personal e-mail system during her time as Secretary of State.

After a tremendous amount of work over the last year, the FBI is completing its investigation and referring the case to the Department of Justice for a prosecutive decision. What I would like to do today is tell you three things: what we did; what we found; and what we are recommending to the Department of Justice.

This will be an unusual statement in at least a couple ways. First, I am going to include more detail about our process than I ordinarily would, because I think the American people deserve those details in a case of intense public interest. Second, I have not coordinated or reviewed this statement in any way with the Department of Justice or any other part of the government. They do not know what I am about to say.

I want to start by thanking the FBI employees who did remarkable work in this case. Once you have a better sense of how much we have done, you will understand why I am so grateful and proud of their efforts.

So, first, what we have done: The investigation began as a referral from the Intelligence Community Inspector General in connection with Secretary Clinton's use of a personal e-mail server during her time as Secretary of State. The referral focused on whether classified information was transmitted on that personal system.

Federal Bureau of Investigation (FBI) press briefing delivered on July 5, 2016, in Washington, DC.

Our investigation looked at whether there is evidence classified information was improperly stored or transmitted on that personal system, in violation of a federal statute making it a felony to mishandle classified information either intentionally or in a grossly negligent way, or a second statute making it a misdemeanor to knowingly remove classified information from appropriate systems or storage facilities.

Consistent with our counterintelligence responsibilities, we have also investigated to determine whether there is evidence of computer intrusion in connection with the personal e-mail server by any foreign power, or other hostile actors.

I have so far used the singular term, "e-mail server," in describing the referral that began our investigation. It turns out to have been more complicated than that. Secretary Clinton used several different servers and administrators of those servers during her four years at the State Department, and used numerous mobile devices to view and send e-mail on that personal domain. As new servers and equipment were employed, older servers were taken out of service, stored, and decommissioned in various ways. Piecing all of that back together—to gain as full an understanding as possible of the ways in which personal e-mail was used for government work—has been a painstaking undertaking, requiring thousands of hours of effort.

For example, when one of Secretary Clinton's original personal servers was decommissioned in 2013, the e-mail software was removed. Doing that didn't remove the e-mail content, but it was like removing the frame from a huge finished jigsaw puzzle and dumping the pieces on the floor. The effect was that millions of e-mail fragments end up unsorted in the server's unused—or "slack"—space. We searched through all of it to see what was there, and what parts of the puzzle could be put back together.

FBI investigators have also read all of the approximately 30,000 e-mails provided by Secretary Clinton to the State Department in December 2014. Where an e-mail was assessed as possibly containing classified information, the FBI referred the e-mail to any U.S. government agency that was a likely "owner" of information in the e-mail, so that agency could make a determination as to whether the e-mail contained classified information at the time it was sent or received, or whether there was reason to classify the e-mail now, even if its content was not classified at the time it was sent (that is the process sometimes referred to as "up-classifying").

From the group of 30,000 e-mails returned to the State Department, 110 e-mails in 52 e-mail chains have been determined by the owning agency to contain classified information at the time they were sent or received. Eight of those chains contained information that was Top Secret at the time they were sent; 36 chains contained Secret information at the time; and eight contained Confidential information, which is the lowest level of classification. Separate from those, about 2,000 additional e-mails were "up-classified" to make them Confidential; the information in those had not been classified at the time the e-mails were sent.

The FBI also discovered several thousand work-related e-mails that were not in the group of 30,000 that were returned by Secretary Clinton to State in 2014. We found those additional e-mails in a variety of ways. Some had been deleted over the years and we found traces of them on devices that supported or were connected to the private e-mail domain. Others we found by reviewing the archived government e-mail accounts of people who had been government employees at the same time as Secretary Clinton, including high-ranking officials at other agencies, people with whom a Secretary of State might naturally correspond.

This helped us recover work-related e-mails that were not among the 30,000 produced to State. Still others we recovered from the laborious review of the millions of e-mail fragments dumped into the slack space of the server decommissioned in 2013.

With respect to the thousands of e-mails we found that were not among those produced to State, agencies have concluded that three of those were classified at the time they were sent or received, one at the Secret level and two at the Confidential level. There were no additional Top Secret e-mails found. Finally, none of those we found have since been "up-classified."

I should add here that we found no evidence that any of the additional work-related e-mails were intentionally deleted in an effort to conceal them. Our assessment is that, like many e-mail users, Secretary Clinton periodically deleted e-mails or e-mails were purged from the system when devices were changed. Because she was not using a government account—or even a commercial account like Gmail—there was no archiving at all of her e-mails, so it is not surprising that we discovered e-mails that were not on Secretary Clinton's system in 2014, when she produced the 30,000 e-mails to the State Department.

It could also be that some of the additional work-related e-mails we recovered were among those deleted as "personal" by Secretary Clinton's lawyers when they reviewed and sorted her e-mails for production in 2014.

The lawyers doing the sorting for Secretary Clinton in 2014 did not individually read the content of all of her e-mails, as we did for those available to us; instead, they relied on header information and used search terms to try to find all work-related e-mails among the reportedly more than 60,000 total e-mails remaining on Secretary Clinton's personal system in 2014. It is highly likely their search terms missed some work-related e-mails, and that we later found them, for example, in the mailboxes of other officials or in the slack space of a server.

It is also likely that there are other work-related e-mails that they did not produce to State and that we did not find elsewhere, and that are now gone because they deleted all e-mails they did not return to State, and the lawyers cleaned their devices in such a way as to preclude complete forensic recovery.

We have conducted interviews and done technical examination to attempt to understand how that sorting was done by her attorneys. Although we do not have complete visibility because we are not able to fully reconstruct the electronic record of that sorting, we believe our investigation has been sufficient to give us reasonable confidence there was no intentional misconduct in connection with that sorting effort.

And, of course, in addition to our technical work, we interviewed many people, from those involved in setting up and maintaining the various iterations of Secretary Clinton's personal server, to staff members with whom she corresponded on e-mail, to those involved in the e-mail production to State, and finally, Secretary Clinton herself.

Last, we have done extensive work to understand what indications there might be of compromise by hostile actors in connection with the personal e-mail operation.

That's what we have done. Now let me tell you what we found: Although we did not find clear evidence that Secretary Clinton or her colleagues intended to violate laws governing the handling of classified information, there is evidence that they were extremely careless in their handling of very sensitive, highly classified information.

For example, seven e-mail chains concern matters that were classified at the Top Secret/Special Access Program level when they were sent and received. These chains involved Secretary Clinton both sending e-mails about those matters and receiving e-mails from others about the same matters. There is evidence to support a conclusion that any reasonable person in Secretary Clinton's position, or in the position of those government employees with whom she was corresponding about these matters, should have known that an unclassified system was no place for that conversation. In addition to this highly sensitive information, we also found information that was properly classified as Secret by the U.S. Intelligence Community at the time it was discussed on e-mail (that is, excluding the later "up-classified" e-mails).

None of these e-mails should have been on any kind of unclassified system, but their presence is especially concerning because all of these e-mails were housed on unclassified personal servers not even supported by full-time security staff, like those found at Departments and Agencies of the U.S. Government—or even with a commercial service like Gmail.

Separately, it is important to say something about the marking of classified information. Only a very small number of the e-mails containing classified information bore markings indicating the presence of classified information. But even if information is not marked "classified" in an e-mail, participants who know or should know that the subject matter is classified are still obligated to protect it.

While not the focus of our investigation, we also developed evidence that the security culture of the State Department in general, and with respect to use of unclassified e-mail systems in particular, was generally lacking in the kind of care for classified information found elsewhere in the government.

With respect to potential computer intrusion by hostile actors, we did not find direct evidence that Secretary Clinton's personal e-mail domain, in its various configurations since 2009, was successfully hacked. But, given the nature of the system and of the actors potentially involved, we assess that we would be unlikely to see such direct evidence. We do assess that hostile actors gained access to the private commercial e-mail accounts of people with whom Secretary Clinton was in regular contact from her personal account. We also assess that Secretary Clinton's use of a personal e-mail domain was both known by a large number of people and readily apparent. She also used her personal e-mail extensively while outside the United States, including sending and receiving work-related e-mails in the territory of sophisticated adversaries. Given that combination of factors, we assess it is possible that hostile actors gained access to Secretary Clinton's personal e-mail account.

So that's what we found. Finally, with respect to our recommendation to the Department of Justice: In our system, the prosecutors make the decisions about whether charges are appropriate based on evidence the FBI has helped collect. Although we don't normally make public our recommendations to the prosecutors, we frequently make recommendations and engage in productive conversations with prosecutors about what resolution may be appropriate, given the evidence. In this case, given the importance of the matter, I think unusual transparency is in order.

Although there is evidence of potential violations of the statutes regarding the handling of classified information, our judgment is that no reasonable prosecutor would bring such a case. Prosecutors necessarily weigh a number of factors before bringing charges. There are obvious considerations, like the strength of the evidence, especially regarding intent. Responsible decisions also consider the context of a person's actions, and how similar situations have been handled in the past.

In looking back at our investigations into mishandling or removal of classified information, we cannot find a case that would support bringing criminal charges on these facts. All the cases prosecuted involved some combination of: clearly intentional and willful mishandling of classified information; or vast quantities of materials exposed in such a way as to support an inference of intentional misconduct; or indications of disloyalty to the United States; or efforts to obstruct justice. We do not see those things here.

To be clear, this is not to suggest that in similar circumstances, a person who engaged in this activity would face no consequences. To the contrary, those individuals are often subject to security or administrative sanctions. But that is not what we are deciding now.

As a result, although the Department of Justice makes final decisions on matters like this, we are expressing to Justice our view that no charges are appropriate in this case.

I know there will be intense public debate in the wake of this recommendation, as there was throughout this investigation. What I can assure the American people is that this investigation was done competently, honestly, and independently. No outside influence of any kind was brought to bear.

I know there were many opinions expressed by people who were not part of the investigation—including people in government—but none of that mattered to us. Opinions are irrelevant, and they were all uninformed by insight into our investigation, because we did the investigation the right way. Only facts matter, and the FBI found them here in an entirely apolitical and professional way. I couldn't be prouder to be part of this organization.

Print Citations

CMS: Comey, James. "Statement on the Clinton E-mail Investigation." Speech presented at an FBI press briefing, Washington, DC, July, 2016. In *The Reference Shelf: Representative American Speeches 2015-2016*, edited by Betsy Maury, 117-22. Ipswich, MA: H.W. Wilson, 2016.

MLA: Comey, James. "Statement on the Clinton E-mail Investigation." FBI press briefing. Washington, DC. July, 2016. Presentation. *The Reference Shelf: Representative American Speeches 2015-2016*. Ed. Betsy Maury. Ipswich: H.W. Wilson, 2016. 117-22. Print.

APA: Comey, J. (2016). Statement on the Clinton e-mail investigation. [Presentation]. *Speech presented at an FBI press briefing*. Washington, DC. In Betsy Maury (Ed.), *The reference shelf: Representative American speeches 2015-2016* (pp. 117-122). Ipswich, MA: H.W. Wilson. (Original work published 2016)

Speech at Our Ocean Conference

By Leonardo DiCaprio

Actor and environmental activist Leonardo DiCaprio spoke about the issues facing oceans at the 2016 Our Ocean Conference in Washington, DC hosted by Secretary of State John Kerry. The Our Ocean Conference focuses on key ocean issues—marine protected areas, sustainable fisheries, marine pollution, and climate-related impacts on the ocean. Leonardo DiCaprio spoke about his experience witnessing the detrimental affects of climate change while filming his documentary Before The Flood. *He also spoke about several new innovative and collaborative solutions that have been developed to address the problems facing our oceans. These include the recent launch of Global Fishing Watch as well as a new initiative to protect sharks and rays called Global Partnership for Sharks and Rays. Leonardo DiCaprio is an Academy Award-winning actor. He heads the Leonardo DiCaprio Foundation, a nonprofit organization dedicated to global conservation.*

Thank you, Secretary Kerry for that kind introduction.

I was with you for the very first "Our Oceans" conference two years ago—and since then, this group, with your visionary leadership, has accomplished so much. This conference has become a true platform for action.

As a group we have galvanized unprecedented action for our oceans, protecting millions of square kilometers, an area more than twice the size of India, we've elevated these issues to a global stage, and we've educated our leaders and the public on how much our climate, food security, economic security, and ultimately our future on this planet depends on the health of our oceans.

It's critical that we keep up this momentum because the future of our oceans continues to be challenged by an astonishing long list of threats. Warming waters, acidification, plastic pollution, methane releases, drilling, overfishing, and the destruction of marine ecosystems like coral reefs are pushing our oceans to the brink.

This year, Australia's Great Barrier Reef suffered what is thought to be the largest bleaching event ever recorded. Over 600 miles of reef, previously teeming with life, is devastated. We are seeing this level of impact to coral reefs around the world: from Hawaii to the Florida Keys, from Madagascar to Indonesia.

I saw this with my own eyes while filming my new documentary *Before the Flood* which chronicles the impacts of climate change. Marine scientist Jeremy Jackson

Delivered on September 15, 2016 at Our Oceans Conference in Washington, DC.

led me underwater in a submersible to observe the reefs off the coast of the Bahamas. What I saw took my breath away—not a fish in sight, colorless, ghost-like coral, a graveyard.

This is the state of the majority of the world's coral reefs and it is a sobering reality. We've destroyed irreplaceable ecosystems, reversing half a billion years of evolution.

I also recently visited Palau and met with the leaders of Kirabas, two island nations in the South Pacific that are feeling the impacts of a warming climate right now. Houses are abandoned because of the rising tides and whole communities face an uncertain future as their islands shrink, waters closing in around them. The nation of Kirabas is already preparing for the unprecedented relocation of their people, having purchased land in Fiji to accommodate an almost certain migration from their home.

These nations are also dependent on the health of the seas for their economic survival. Tuna is the number one source of income for Kiribas. To prevent a collapse of this fishery, Kiribas created a marine protected area the size of California. They understand that protecting nature, giving it a chance to rebound and replenish, is the key to protecting the future of their nation, their culture, and their people.

We need more leaders and communities to take bold actions like this. As a global community we must protect and value vital marine ecosystems, rather than treating the oceans as an endless resource to be exploited and as a dumping ground for our waste.

Oceans absorb about a third of the carbon that we pump into the atmosphere but we've pushed too far, the ocean can no longer keep up with our rampant rate of carbon dioxide emissions. Today our seas are warmer and far more acidic, weakening the shells of marine creatures and destroying coral reefs that we all depend on for life.

The only way we can avert disaster is by innovating, implementing, and scaling up the solutions to these problems as quickly as possible.

One solution that is poised to address global overfishing and illegal fishing is the new platform Global Fishing Watch. This innovative technology is the result of a powerful partnership that leverages the unique skills of each participating organization: Google's ability to organize big data and information and make it universally accessible, SkyTruth's ability to use satellites to monitor threats to the planet, and Oceana's ability to execute winning campaigns to bring back fishery abundance.

Today, this unprecedented technology is available to everyone in the world. I encourage you to check it out, here in the Watch Room and on your own devices as soon as you can at globalfishingwatch.org.

This platform will empower citizens across the globe to become powerful advocates for our oceans. With the data Global Fishing Watch provides, governments, fishery management organizations, researchers and the fishing industry can work together to rebuild fisheries and protect critical marine habitats. We encourage all of you to take advantage of this new technology and work together to effectively monitor and protect our seas.

Another critical issue is the global crisis facing sharks and rays. In recent years, markets for shark fin, liver oil, cartilage, leather, meat, and ray gill plates have surged, while conservation efforts have failed to keep pace. As a result it is estimated that 100 million sharks are killed annually, with over 90% population declines for some species, and nearly a quarter of all species are now facing extinction.

The Global Partnership for Sharks and Rays is a coalition working to halt the over-exploitation of these species, reverse their decline, restore populations, and prevent extinctions. This collaborative effort which is close to me personally is also supported by the Paul M. Angel Foundation, the Helmsley Charitable Trust, Oceans 5, and the Paul G. Allen Family Foundation. We joined together to develop a global strategy to stop the slaughter of sharks and rays and to ramp-up resources to change the tide for these incredible species.

These initiatives are great examples of what can be achieved when the right partners come together to solve challenging problems.

There are many other exciting solutions and game changing commitments that will be shared over the next two days. Among them are President Obama's incredible announcement just a few weeks ago to create the largest protected area on the planet in and around the Northwestern Hawaiian Islands. And then again today the President announced the Northeast Canyons and Seamounts Marine National Monument, an important marine ecosystem off the coast of Cape Cod.

This is exactly the kind of bold leadership we need more of.

I am truly inspired by this group and all that you have collectively done to protect our oceans since the first conference two years ago but my hope is that this is just the beginning.

The great ocean explorer Jacques Cousteau said, "The sea, once it casts its spell, holds one in its' net of wonder forever." That is true for me. I suspect it is true for each of you. But there will be no wonders for our children and grandchildren to behold unless we step up and push ourselves to go bigger, to be bolder, to take action now to protect our oceans before it's too late.

Thank you.

Print Citations

CMS: DiCaprio, Leonardo. "Speech at Our Ocean Conference." Speech presented at Our Ocean Conference, Washington, DC, September, 2016. In *The Reference Shelf: Representative American Speeches 2015-2016*, edited by Betsy Maury, 123-25. Ipswich, MA: H.W. Wilson, 2016.

MLA: DiCaprio, Leonardo. "Speech at Our Ocean Conference." Speech presented at Our Ocean Conference, Washington, DC. September, 2016. Presentation. *The Reference Shelf: Representative American Speeches 2015-2016*. Ed. Betsy Maury. Ipswich: H.W. Wilson, 2016. 123-25. Print.

APA: DiCaprio, L. (2016). Speech at our ocean conference. [Presentation]. *Speech presented at Our Ocean Conference*. Washington, DC. In Betsy Maury (Ed.), *The reference shelf: Representative American speeches 2015-2016* (pp. 123-125). Ipswich, MA: H.W. Wilson. (Original work published 2016)

Remarks After Briefing on the Attack in Orlando, Florida

By Barack Obama

In this speech after the mass shooting at a gay nightclub in Orlando, Florida, President Barack Obama speaks to the press about the ongoing investigation, calling the massacre an act of terrorism. The president is asked about the perpetrator, his connections to ISIL, and the nature of hate crimes against the LGBT community. He uses the opportunity to call for stricter gun regulation and also raises the issue of dealing with home-grown terrorism on American soil. Barack Obama is the 44th president of the United States, having been elected to office in 2008 and reelected in 2012. Prior to becoming president, Obama was a United States senator representing Illinois from 2005 to 2008.

THE PRESIDENT: I just had the opportunity to get the latest briefing from FBI Director Comey, as well as Deputy Attorney General Yates and the rest of my national security team about the tragedy that took place in Orlando. They're going to be doing a more extensive briefing around noon—just a little bit after noon over at FBI headquarters. So I will allow them to go into all the details, but I thought it was important for you to hear directly from me.

First of all, our hearts go out to the families of those who have been killed. Our prayers go to those who have been wounded. This is a devastating attack on all Americans. It is one that is particularly painful for the people of Orlando, but I think we all recognize that this could have happened anywhere in this country. And we feel enormous solidarity and grief on behalf of the families that have been affected.

The fact that it took place at a club frequented by the LGBT community I think is also relevant. We're still looking at all the motivations of the killer. But it's a reminder that regardless of race, religion, faith or sexual orientation, we're all Americans, and we need to be looking after each other and protecting each other at all times in the face of this kind of terrible act.

With respect to the killer, there's been a lot of reporting that's been done. It's important to emphasize that we're still at the preliminary stages of the investigation, and there's a lot more that we have to learn. The one thing that we can say is that this is being treated as a terrorist investigation. It appears that the shooter was inspired by various extremist information that was disseminated over the Internet. All those

Delivered on June 13, 2016, in Washington, DC.

materials are currently being searched, exploited so we will have a better sense of the pathway that the killer took in making the decision to launch this attack.

As Director Comey I think will indicate, at this stage we see no clear evidence that he was directed externally. It does appear that, at the last minute, he announced allegiance to ISIL, but there is no evidence so far that he was in fact directed by ISIL. And there also at this stage is no direct evidence that he was part of a larger plot. In that sense, it appears to be similar to what we saw in San Bernardino, but we don't yet know. And this is part of what is going to be important in terms of the investigation.

As far as we can tell right now, this is certainly an example of the kind of homegrown extremism that all of us have been so concerned about for a very long time. It also appears that he was able to obtain these weapons legally because he did not have a criminal record that, in some ways, would prohibit him from purchasing these weapons. It appears that one of those weapons he was able to just carry out of the store—an assault rifle, a handgun—a Glock—which had a lot of clips in it. He was apparently required to wait for three days under Florida law. But it does indicate the degree to which it was not difficult for him to obtain these kinds of weapons.

Director Comey will discuss the fact that there had been some investigation of him in the past that was triggered, but as Director Comey I think will indicate, the FBI followed the procedures that they were supposed to and did a proper job.

At the end of the day, this is something that we are going to have to grapple with—making sure that even as we go after ISIL and other extremist organizations overseas, even as we hit their leadership, even as we go after their infrastructure, even as we take key personnel off the field, even as we disrupt external plots—that one of the biggest challenges we are going to have is this kind of propaganda and perversions of Islam that you see generated on the Internet, and the capacity for that to seep into the minds of troubled individuals or weak individuals, and seeing them motivated then to take actions against people here in the United States and elsewhere in the world that are tragic. And so countering this extremist ideology is increasingly going to be just as important as making sure that we are disrupting more extensive plots engineered from the outside.

We are also going to have to have to make sure that we think about the risks we are willing to take by being so lax in how we make very powerful firearms available to people in this country. And this is something that obviously I've talked about for a very long time.

My concern is that we start getting into a debate, as has happened in the past, which is an either/or debate. And the suggestion is either we think about something as terrorism and we ignore the problems with easy access to firearms, or it's all about firearms and we ignore the role—the very real role that that organizations like ISIL have in generating extremist views inside this country. And it's not an either/or. It's a both/and.

We have to go after these terrorist organizations and hit them hard. We have to counter extremism. But we also have to make sure that it is not easy for somebody who decides they want to harm people in this country to be able to obtain weapons to get at them.

And my hope is, is that over the next days and weeks that we are being sober about how we approach this problem, that we let the facts get determined by our investigators, but we also do some reflecting in terms of how we can best tackle what is going to be a very challenging problem not just here in this country, but around the world.

Again, my final point is just to extend our deepest sympathies to the families of those who were affected and to send our prayers to those who are surviving and are in hospitals right now, and their family members hoping that they get better very soon.

But in the meantime, you can anticipate sometime around noon that Director Comey and Deputy Attorney General Yates will provide you with a more full briefing about this. Okay?

QUESTION: Mr. President, is there anything more to the LBGT angle to this?

THE PRESIDENT: Well, I think we don't yet know the motivations. But here's what we do know—is organizations like ISIL or organizations like al Qaeda, or those who have perverted Islam and created these radical, nihilistic, vicious organizations, one of the groups that they target are gays and lesbians because they believe that they do not abide by their attitudes towards sexuality.

Now, we also know these are organizations that think it's fine to take captive women and enslave them and rape them. So there clearly are connections between the attitudes in an organization like this and their attitudes towards tolerance and pluralism and a belief that all people are created equally regardless of sexual orientation. That is something threatening to them. Women being empowered is threatening to them.

So, yes, I'm sure we will find that there are connections—regardless of the particular motivations of this killer—there are connections between this vicious, bankrupt ideology and general attitudes towards gays and lesbians. And unfortunately, that's something that the LGBT community is subject to not just by ISIL but by a lot of groups that purport to speak on behalf of God around the world.

QUESTION: What are your thoughts about the fact that after all of these incidents over these years, that there has not been any move to reform gun control in this country?

THE PRESIDENT: April, I think you know what I think about it. The fact that we make it this challenging for law enforcement, for example, even to get alerted that somebody who they are watching has purchased a gun—and if they do get alerted, sometimes it's hard for them to stop them from getting a gun—is crazy. It's a problem. And we have to, I think, do some soul-searching.

But again, the danger here is, is that then it ends up being the usual political debate. And the NRA and the gun control folks say that, oh, Obama doesn't want to talk about terrorism. And if you talk about terrorism, then people say why aren't you looking at issues of gun control.

The point is, is that if we have self-radicalized individuals in this country, then they are going to be very difficult oftentimes to find ahead of time. And how easy it is for them to obtain weapons is, in some cases, going to make a difference as to whether they're able to carry out attacks like this or not. And we make it very easy for individuals who are troubled or disturbed or want to engage in violent acts to get very powerful weapons very quickly. And that's a problem.

It's a problem regardless of their motivations. It's a problem for a young man who can walk into a church in South Carolina and murder nine people who offered to pray with him. It's a problem when an angry young man on a college campus decides to shoot people because he feels disrespected. It's certainly a problem when we have organizations like ISIL or al Qaeda who are actively trying to promote violence and are doing so very effectively over the Internet, because we know that at some point there are going to be, out of 300 million, there are going to be some individuals who find for whatever reason that kind of horrible propaganda enticing. And if that happens, and that person can get a weapon, that's a problem.

Print Citations

CMS: Obama, Barack. "Remarks After Briefing on the Attack in Orlando, Florida." Washington, DC, June, 2016. In *The Reference Shelf: Representative American Speeches 2015-2016*, edited by Betsy Maury, 127-30. Ipswich, MA: H.W. Wilson, 2016.

MLA: Obama, Barack. "Remarks After Briefing on the Attack in Orlando, Florida." Washington, DC. June, 2016. Presentation. *The Reference Shelf: Representative American Speeches 2015-2016*. Ed. Betsy Maury. Ipswich: H.W. Wilson, 2016. 127-30. Print.

APA: Obama, B. (2016). Remarks after briefing on the attack in Orlando, Florida. [Presentation]. Washington, DC. In Betsy Maury (Ed.), *The reference shelf: Representative American speeches 2015-2016* (pp. 127-130). Ipswich, MA: Salem. (Original work published 2016)

Love Is Love

By Lin-Manuel Miranda

Lin-Manuel Miranda won the award for Best Score for Hamilton *at the 2016 Tony Awards, where his original musical swept the awards with 11 wins. In lieu of a traditional acceptance speech, the* Hamilton *creator and star—hours after the mass shooting in Orlando—delivered a beautifully composed sonnet. The poem, performed in Miranda's rapid-fire verse, seemed intended as a love poem to his wife, Vanessa, as well as an elegy for those killed in the tragedy in Orlando. Lin-Manuel Miranda is an American actor, composer, rapper, and writer, best known for creating and starring in the Broadway musicals* Hamilton *and* In the Heights. *He has won a Pulitzer Prize, two Grammys, an Emmy, a MacArthur "Genius" Award, and three Tony awards, among others.*

My wife's the reason anything gets done.

She nudges me towards promise by degrees.

She is a perfect symphony of one, our son is her most beautiful reprise.

We chase the melodies that seem to find us

until they're finished songs and start to play.

When senseless acts of tragedy remind us

that nothing here is promised, not one day.

This show is proof that history remembers.

We live through times when hate and fear seem stronger.

We rise and fall and light from dying embers.

Remembrances that hope and love live longer.

And love is love is love is love is love is love cannot be killed or swept aside.

As sacred as a symphony, Eliza tells her story and fills the world with music love and pride.

Thank you so much for this.

Delivered on June 12, 2016 at the Beacon Theatre in New York, New York.

Print Citations

CMS: Miranda, Lin-Manuel. "Love Is Love." Speech presented at the Beacon Theatre, New York, New York, June, 2016. In *The Reference Shelf: Representative American Speeches 2015-2016*, edited by Betsy Maury, 131. Ipswich, MA: H.W. Wilson, 2016

MLA: Miranda, Lin-Manuel. "Love Is Love." Beacon Theatre. New York, NY. June, 2016. Presentation. *The Reference Shelf: Representative American Speeches 2015-2016*. Ed. Betsy Maury. Ipswich: H.W. Wilson, 2016. 131. Print.

APA: Miranda, L.-M. (2016). Love is love. [Presentation]. *Speech presented at the Beacon Theatre*. New York, NY. In Betsy Maury (Ed.), *The reference shelf: Representative American speeches 2015-2016* (p. 131). Ipswich, MA: H.W. Wilson. (Original work published 2016)

"I'll Continue to Sit"

By Colin Kaepernick

In this transcript Colin Kaepernick, the San Francisco 49ers quarterback explains his reasons for sitting during the playing of the national anthem. He spoke for 18 minutes and answered questions about his controversial stance. Kaepernick's actions sparked controversy throughout the NFL and led to heated discussions about civil disobedience, racial injustice, and the role of celebrities and athletes in drawing attention to questions of social and racial justice.

Why did you choose to do this?

People don't realize what's really going on in this country. There are a lot things that are going on that are unjust. People aren't being held accountable for. And that's something that needs to change. That's something that this country stands for freedom, liberty and justice for all. And it's not happening for all right now.

Is this something that's evolved in your mind?

It's something that I've seen, I've felt, wasn't quite sure how to deal with originally. And it is something that's evolved. It's something that as I've gained more knowledge about, what's gone in this country in the past, what's going on currently. These aren't new situations. This isn't new ground. There are things that have gone on in this country for years and years and have never been addressed, and they need to be.

Will you continue to sit?

Yes. I'll continue to sit. I'm going to continue to stand with the people that are being oppressed. To me this is something that has to change. When there's significant change and I feel like that flag represents what it's supposed to represent, this country is representing people the way that it's supposed to, I'll stand.

(inaudible)

There's a lot of things that need to change. One specifically? Police brutality. There's people being murdered unjustly and not being held accountable. People are being given paid leave for killing people. That's not right. That's not right by anyone's standards.

So many people see the flag as a symbol of the military. How do you view it and what do you say to those people?

I have great respect for the men and women that have fought for this country. I have family, I have friends that have gone and fought for this country. And they fight for freedom, they fight for the people, they fight for liberty and justice, for everyone. That's not happening. People are dying in vain because this country isn't holding their end of the bargain up, as far as giving freedom and justice, liberty to everybody. That's something that's not happening. I've seen videos, I've seen circumstances where men and women that have been in the military have come back and been treated unjustly by the country they fought have for, and have been murdered by the country they fought for, on our land. That's not right.

Do you personally feel oppressed?

There have been situations where I feel like I've been ill-treated, yes. This stand wasn't for me. This stand wasn't because I feel like I'm being put down in any kind of way. This is because I'm seeing things happen to people that don't have a voice, people that don't have a platform to talk and have their voices heard, and effect change. So I'm in the position where I can do that and I'm going to do that for people that can't.

Is this the first year that you've sat during the anthem?

This year's the first year that I've done this.

All the preseason games so far?

Yes.

(inaudible)

The support I've gotten from my teammates has been great. I think a lot of my teammates come from areas where this might be the situation. Their families might be put in this situation. It's something that I've had a lot of people come up to me and say, "I really respect you for what you're doing and what you're standing for." So to me that's something that I know what I'm doing was right and I know other people see what I'm doing is right, it's something that we have to come together. We have to unite. We have to unify and make a change.

(inaudible)

I don't understand how it's the wrong way. To me, this is a freedom that we're allowed in this country. And going back to the military, it's a freedom that men and women that have fought for this country have given me this opportunity by contributions they have made. So I don't see it as going about it the wrong way. This is something that has to be said, it has to be brought to the forefront of everyone's attention, and when that's done, I think people can realize what the situation is and then really effect change.

(Inaudible)

It wasn't something that I really planned as far as it blowing up. It was something that I personally decided—I just can't stand what this represents right now. It's not right. And the fact that it has blown up like this, I think it's a good thing. It brings awareness. Everybody knows what's going on and this sheds more light on it. Now, I think people are really talking about it. Having conversations about how to make change. What's really going on this country. And we can move forward.

Are you concerned that this can be seen as a blanket indictment of law enforcement in general?

There is police brutality. People of color have been targeted by police. So that's a large part of it and they're government officials. They are put in place by the government. So that's something that this country has to change. There's things we can do to hold them more accountable. Make those standards higher. You have people that practice law and are lawyers and go to school for eight years, but you can become a cop in six months and don't have to have the same amount of training as a cosmetologist. That's insane. Someone that's holding a curling iron has more education and more training than people that have a gun and are going out on the street to protect us.

Do you plan to do things beyond sitting during the national anthem, as far as activism?

Yeah, most definitely. There are things that I have in the works right now that I'm working on to put together in the future and have come to fruition soon. Those are things that I'll talk about as we get closer to those days.

Any concern about the timing of this and the possibility of it being a distraction?

No, I don't see it being a distraction. It's something that can unify this team. It's something that can unify this country. If we have these real conversations that are uncomfortable for a lot of people. If we have these conversations, there's a better understanding of where both sides are coming from. And if we reach common ground, and can understand what everybody's going through, we can really effect change. And make sure that everyone is treated equally and has the same freedom.

Has anyone from the NFL or team asked you to tone it down? It doesn't seem as if anyone is trying to quiet you.

No. No one's tried to quiet me and, to be honest, it's not something I'm going to be quiet about. I'm going to speak the truth when I'm asked about it. This isn't for looks. This isn't for publicity or anything like that. This is for people that don't have the voice. And this is for people that are being oppressed and need to have equal opportunities to be successful. To provide for families and not live in poor circumstances.

In your mind have you been pulled over unjustly or had bad experiences?

Yes, multiple times. I've had times where one of my roommates was moving out of the house in college and because we were the only black people in that neighborhood the cops got called and we had guns drawn on us. Came in the house, without knocking, guns drawn on my teammates and roommates. So I have experienced this. People close to me have experienced this. This isn't something that's a one-off case here or a one-off case there. This has become habitual. This has become a habit. So this is something that needs to be addressed.

Colin, you're the only player in the NFL taking this stand. Why do you think you're the only one doing this?

I think there's a lot of consequences that come along with this. There's a lot of people that don't want to have this conversation. They're scared they might lose their job. Or they might not get the endorsements. They might not to be treated the same way. Those are things I'm prepared to handle. Things that other people might not be ready for. It's just a matter of where you're at in your life. Where your mind's at. At this point, I've been blessed to be able to get this far and have the privilege of being able to be in the NFL, making the kind of money I make and enjoy luxuries like that. I can't look in the mirror and see people dying on the street that should have the same opportunities that I've had. And say "You know what? I can live with myself." Because I can't if I just watch.

Do you think you might get cut over this?

I don't know. But if I do, I know I did what's right. And I can live with that at the end of the day.

Does this have anything to do with your relationship with the 49ers or the NFL?

No, this is about the way people have been treated by this country.

How long did you talk when you addressed the team?

It was a conversation. They asked me to talk and just explain why I did what I did. And why I felt the way I felt. I had an open conversation with them. I told them why I felt that way and looked at things the way I do. A lot of it has to do with the history of the country and where we're currently at. I opened it up to all my teammates. Come talk to me if you have any questions. If you want to understand what I'm thinking further, come talk to me. It shouldn't be something that should be hidden. These conversations need to happen and can bring everybody closer.

Were there people that disagreed?

There were people that said I want to understand further. Let's talk. So I've had those conversations and will continue to have them with my teammates. It's something that—the knowledge of what's happened in this country and what's currently happening, I think everybody needs to know. And when you have the knowledge of those things you can make an educated decision on what you really feel and what you really stand for.

Have you had people outside the sports world reach out to say they support you?

I've had a few people reach out. Quite a few, actually. Saying—we really support you. We're proud of you for taking a stand. We respect what you're doing. We know a lot is going to come with it, but we're behind you. And that means a lot. That means I'm not the only one who feels this way and I'm not the only one who sees things this way.

Is the team talking about football or this?

No, we're focused on football while we're in meetings, while we're on the field. That's what our focus is. But in our free time, we have conversations about this. That's not something that we should be ashamed about or shy away from. We talked about football, we handled our business there but there's also a social responsibility that we have to be educated on these things and talk about these things.

Consider getting teammates to join?

This isn't something I'm going to ask other people to put their necks out for what I'm doing. If they agree with me and feel strongly about it then by all means I hope they stand with me. But I'm not going to go and try to recruit people and be like "Hey, come do this with me" because I know the consequences that come with that and they need to make that decision for themselves.

Reach out to anyone before this?

This is a conversation I've had with a lot of people a lot of times over a long period of time so it wasn't something that I planned on having a conversation about at a particular time. It just so happened it was the other night that people realized it and talked about it.

Any concern that the focus is on you and not the issues?

I do think that the talk has been more about me, more about I know a lot of people's initial reactions thought it was bashing the military, which it wasn't. That wasn't my intention at all. I think now that we have those things cleared up, we can get to the root of what I was saying and really address those issues.

Any other players who feel the same but are not ready to step forward publicly?

Yeah, I know there's other players that feel the same way. I've had other players reach out to me. Once again, it's not something I'm going to ask them to put their necks out. I know the consequences that come along with my decision and if they feel strongly and want to stand with me, then I hope they do. If it's something they're not ready for then that's what the conversations are for and they can make that decision when they're ready or if they're ready.

Fear for your safety on the road?

Not really too concerned about that. At the end of the day, if something happens, that's only proving my point.

Has Dr. Harry Edwards been helpful?

Once again, it wasn't something I consulted anybody on. It was a conversation I had when someone asked me about it. Dr. Edwards is a good friend, he's someone I talk to a lot and run things by and have a lot of conversations with and we have a lot of similar views.

Election year have anything to do with timing of this?

It wasn't a timing thing, it wasn't something that was planned. But I think the two presidential candidates that we currently have also represent the issues that we have in this country right now.

Do you want to expand on that?

You have Hillary who has called black teens or black kids super predators, you have Donald Trump who's openly racist. We have a presidential candidate who has deleted emails and done things illegally and is a presidential candidate. That doesn't make sense to me because if that was any other person you'd be in prison. So, what is this country really standing for?

It is a country that has elected a black president twice...

It has elected a black president but there are also a lot of things that haven't changed. There are a lot of issues that still haven't been addressed and that's something over an 8-year term there's a lot of those things are hard to change and there's a lot of those things that he doesn't necessarily have complete control over.

What would be a success?

That's a tough question because there's a lot of things that need to change, a lot of different issues that need to be addressed. That's something that it's really hard to lock down one specific thing that needs to change currently.

Print Citations

CMS: Kaepernick, Colin. "I'll Continue to Sit." Speech presented in the *San Francisco Chronicle*, August, 2016. In *The Reference Shelf: Representative American Speeches 2015-2016*, edited by Betsy Maury, 133-38. Ipswich, MA: H.W. Wilson, 2016.

MLA: Kaepernick, Colin. "I'll Continue to Sit." *San Francisco Chronicle*. August, 2016. *The Reference Shelf: Representative American Speeches 2015-2016*. Ed. Betsy Maury. Ipswich: H.W. Wilson, 2016. 133-38. Print.

APA: Kaepernick, C. (2016). I'll continue to sit. *San Francisco Chronicle*. In Betsy Maury (Ed.), *The reference shelf: Representative American speeches 2015-2016* (pp. 133-138). Ipswich, MA: H.W. Wilson. (Original work published 2016)

Countering False Narratives

By Peter Salovey

In his freshmen address to the class of 2020, Yale President Peter Salovey welcomes new students to campus and speaks to them about false narratives. He uses the address to talk about the need to be watchful against exaggerations and distortions that serve to fuel fear and anger. President Salovey makes a veiled reference here to the struggles the university had in 2016 with "cultural appropriation" and freedom of speech, which led to the resignation of two residential college professors who championed the wearing of any Halloween costumes. Their stance provoked outrage from undergraduates who charged the professors with insensitivity and demanded their ouster. Peter Salovey is the current president of Yale University. He previously served as Yale's provost, dean of Yale Graduate School of Arts and Sciences, and dean of Yale College.

Good morning and welcome: to my colleagues here on stage, to the family members who have joined us today, and—especially—to the Yale College Class of 2020.

Twenty-twenty—a term that inevitably brings to mind perfect eyesight. And now that all of you are wearing 2020 as your class label in Yale College, I am confident your intuition and your mental acuity will develop here to an equivalent level of strength. The admissions office assures me that everything possible has been done to guarantee this outcome.

Nonetheless, I'd like to reflect—on your "first day of school"—about what might impede your insight and what might advance it in the course of your education here.

For many years, I taught introductory psychology to large numbers of freshmen. In the part of the course devoted to social psychology, I would ask my students to consider what we know about helping others in various kinds of social situations. Specifically, why is it that we offer assistance, or fail to offer assistance, in emergencies?

I would begin with the tragic and well known case of Kitty Genovese, a twenty-nine-year-old woman who lived in Kew Gardens, Queens, and was murdered there in 1964. Her case received enormous attention and commentary, and you have probably heard some version of her story. As reported in the *New York Times*, thirty-eight individuals watched the murder from their apartment windows, but only one called the police, and by then it was too late.

Over the years, I have described this shocking incident many times. So have other social psychologists teaching similar courses, and so did the social scientists who

Delivered Saturday, August 27, 2016 in New Haven, Connecticut sought to explain how witnesses could exhibit such callous indifference to a horrific crime taking place before their eyes.

Here's the trouble: the standard account of the Kitty Genovese case is wrong in some of its crucial details.

Kitty's brother, Bill Genovese, produced a film last year called *The Witness*. In it, he documents that some bystanders were not indifferent: one witness shouted out the window at the attacker, another witness held Kitty in her arms as she died, and several called the police during the attack.

So what does it mean that social scientists have been retelling an incorrect version of this story for over fifty years as a paradigmatic example of extreme bystander indifference? Well, among other things, it means that inadvertently we have been perpetuating what could rightly be called a *false narrative*—a version of events that, while partly true, had been shaped, in this case by a newspaper report, to elicit strong negative emotions like anger, fear, or disgust.

As an investigator of human emotions, I know that even the most negative feelings can be important to our survival. Anger effectively signals that a goal is being blocked. Fear motivates caution and preparation. Disgust moves us away from things that can make us ill. However, sometimes our friends, family members, politicians, advertisers, pundits, and others look to manipulate our emotions for their own purposes. Anger, fear, and disgust can be highly effective ways to drive eyeballs to websites, consumers to products, or voters to the polls.

My sense is that we are bombarded daily by false narratives of various kinds, and that they are doing a great deal of damage. In a national election season, you do not need to look very hard to find them.

It is not my purpose today to mock the biggest "whoppers" or award "Pinocchios" for the biggest distortions. Rather, I am only hoping to persuade you that advocates on any side of a question can be tempted to exaggerate or distort or neglect crucial facts in ways that serve primarily to fuel your anger, fear, or disgust.

If I am correct, then an important aspect of your education here will be learning how to recognize and address these kinds of accounts. In the course of that, you should pay especially close attention to the narratives that seem to align best with your own beliefs. To the extent you hold strong political or cultural or religious or economic beliefs, you will simply be like all the rest of us if you gravitate toward explanations that seem to provide confirmation for those beliefs or to demonize those who hold different ones. All of us are strongly predisposed to accept accounts that align with the opinions we already hold, and to ignore or dismiss those that do not. Social media, the blogosphere, and the political process are increasingly drenched with such narratives, inflaming our negative emotions and presenting real barriers to reasoned investigation, productive exchanges between differing views, and the search for common ground on the most challenging problems facing our global societies.

So, you are now embarking on an ambitious and hopeful effort to understand the world, your place in it, and what you can contribute to forward progress. How can you address the seductive power of false narratives, especially in a time when grave mistrust on many sides seems to be fueling ever more of them?

It will not surprise you that I am highly aware of false narratives circulating about students like yourselves and higher education in general. I have a thick shelf of contemporary books assuring me that students at elite universities are merely excellent sheep, that a liberal arts degree is a ticket to unemployment, that truly inspired and courageous learners drop out of college to found tech companies, that millennials cannot make decisions without consulting their parents, that college professors have uniform political views, that students these days are fragile hothouse flowers, that it is not possible to achieve an inclusive campus culture without giving up on free speech, and that our colleges and universities are cut off from reality.

In response, I want to claim that your Yale education will not only enlarge your imagination, advance your knowledge, and propel your career, but also that it will be absolutely critical to your capacity for playing a positive, leadership role in these increasingly polarized and fractious times. In particular, you are about to be taught by outstanding teachers and mentors, whose lives and careers constitute a powerful witness for the value of a disciplined, reasoned, and careful search for light and truth.

What unites our faculty (from engineering to economics to English to environmental studies) is a stubborn skepticism about narratives that oversimplify issues, inflame the emotions, or misdirect the mind. No one is free of biases, of course, but as a community of scholars we subscribe to the ideal of judicious, searching inquiry in the service of reasoned discourse about the matters we investigate and care about the most. We would be lost as academics without this ideal, and our global societies would be lost if universities stopped being places defined by this ideal.

I could supply you with a long list of the Yale faculty who have spent decades of their lives in laboratories, archives, libraries, and field settings collecting evidence to challenge some received notion, some distorted narrative, or some common wisdom that turned out to be highly questionable. Here are some examples:

- Many people assume that our legal system was built almost entirely on a secular tradition. But Yale's professor of medieval history, Anders Winroth, counters the false narrative that contemporary legal reasoning is a radical departure from medieval canon law by showing that in many ways it is rooted in it.

- Important cosmologies of the past depended on the assumption that the planet Earth is unique in the universe. Astronomy professor Debra Fischer has discovered many "worlds" (called exoplanets) orbiting around "suns" in solar systems spread throughout our galaxy.

- Medical researchers assumed for many years that gender has little to do with the prevalence and course of most illnesses, and that findings from studies with men automatically generalize to women. Carolyn Mazure, the director of the Women's Health Research Center at Yale, has been investigating critical differences that gender makes in a wide range of biological systems and translates those findings into new health practices.

- Most classically trained economists have modeled human decisions as the result of careful calculations of costs and benefits. Nobel Prize winner Robert Shiller has emerged at the forefront of those who challenge the idea of rational individuals and markets, forcing major revisions to the theory of human behavior on which his field is based.

- When I was a graduate student in psychology, the dominant narrative held that humans learn virtually everything from experience. But psychology professor Karen Wynn has been teaching us that human infants have surprising innate capacities. Five-month olds appear able to make rudimentary arithmetic calculations. And psychology professor Laurie Santos, the new head of Silliman College, has been showing us that monkeys, too, seem pre-wired for such complex states as resentment, envy, and cognitive dissonance.

- I will close my list of examples by referencing professor of African American and American studies Hazel Carby. Her first book, *Reconstructing Womanhood*, was an exceptional exploration of the ways in which 19th century black women writers in America confronted and transformed the domestic and literary ideals of womanhood in white society. Professor Carby wrote a telling remark in her foreword to a book called *Silencing the Past*, highlighting the power of challenging false or incomplete narratives about the marginalized: "We learn how scanty evidence can be repositioned to generate new narratives, how silences can be made to speak for themselves. . ."

People naturally construct narratives to make sense of their world. I have been concerned to point out that in times of great stress, false narratives may dominate the public mind and public discourse, inflaming negative emotions and fanning discord. In our times especially, a wide array of instantaneous transmissions rapidly amplify such narratives. As a result, we sometimes find that anger, fear, or disgust can blind us to the complexity of the world and the responsibility to seek deeper understandings of important issues.

One point of your Yale education, then, is for you to become a more careful and critical thinker—to learn the difficult, painstaking skills you will need in order to evaluate evidence, to deliberate more broadly and more carefully, and to arrive at your own conclusions.

More particularly, Yale is a place for you to learn how and why to gravitate toward people who view things differently than you do, who will test your most strongly held assumptions. It is also a place to learn why it takes extraordinary discipline, courage, and persistence—often over a lifetime—to construct new foundations for tackling the most intractable and challenging questions of our time. You have come to a place where civil disagreements and deep rethinking are the heart and soul of the enterprise, where we prize exceptional diversity of views alongside the greatest possible freedom of expression.

So I trust that you will begin immediately to seek out what is best about this place: the faculty and staff and peers who will both inspire you and prepare you to become the investigators, visionaries, and leaders the world so sorely needs.

None of us here can hope for a better world, or even for a more inclusive and exhilarating learning community at Yale, unless we succeed at this mission. You are in fact what gives us hope. You are why we became educators. You are why we are here.

Welcome to Yale!

Print Citations

CMS: Salovey, Peter. "Countering False Narratives." New Haven, CT, August, 2016. In *The Reference Shelf: Representative American Speeches 2015-2016*, edited by Betsy Maury, 140-44. Ipswich, MA: H.W. Wilson, 2016.

MLA: Salovey, Peter. "Countering False Narratives." New Haven, CT. August, 2016. Presentation. *The Reference Shelf: Representative American Speeches 2015-2016*. Ed. Betsy Maury. Ipswich: H.W. Wilson, 2016. 140-44. Print.

APA: Salovey, P. (2016). Countering false narratives. [Presentation]. New Haven, CT. In Betsy Maury (Ed.), *The reference shelf: Representative American speeches 2015-2016* (pp. 140-144). Ipswich, MA: H.W. Wilson. (Original work published 2016)

Remarks by the First Lady at a "Hillary for America" Event in New Hampshire

By Michelle Obama

In this campaign speech for Hillary Clinton, Michelle Obama begins speaking about the importance of her initiative Let Girls Learn, and uses the theme of empowering girls to condemn the treatment of women by Republican candidate Donald Trump. Days before this speech an audiotape revealed Trump speaking about women in highly demeaning and disrespectful ways. In a very personal speech, Mrs. Obama talks about the importance of example setting in a president and chronicles Hillary Clinton's life-long commitment to public service. Michelle Obama became First Lady of the United States in 2008. Before her husband was elected to office, Obama worked for the University of Chicago Medical Center and was a member of the staff of Chicago mayor, Richard M Daley. As First Lady, Obama has focused on veteran family issues, LGBT rights, girls' access to education, and childhood health.

MRS. OBAMA: My goodness! (Applause.) You guys are fired up! (Applause.) Well, let me just say hello, everyone. (Applause.) I am so thrilled to be here with you all today in New Hampshire. This is like home to me, and this day—thank you for a beautiful fall day. You just ordered this day up for me, didn't you? (Applause.) It's great to be here.

Let me start by thanking your fabulous governor, your next U.S. senator, Maggie Hassan. (Applause.) I want to thank her for that lovely introduction. I also want to recognize your Congresswoman, Annie McKlane Kuster, who's a dear, dear friend. (Applause.) Your soon-to-be Congresswoman once again, Carol Shea Porter— (applause)—all of whom have been just terrific friends to us. And your Executive Council and candidate for governor, Colin Van Ostern. (Applause.)

And, of course, thanks to all of you for taking the time to be here today. (Applause.)

AUDIENCE MEMBER: We love you! (Applause.)

MRS. OBAMA: Thanks so much. That's very sweet of you. I love you guys too. I can't believe it's just a few weeks before Election Day, as we come together to support the next President and Vice President of the United States, Hillary Clinton and Tim Kaine! (Applause.) And New Hampshire is going to be important, as always.

Delivered on October 13, 2016, at Southern New Hampshire University in Manchester, New Hampshire.

So I'm going to get a little serious here, because I think we can all agree that this has been a rough week in an already rough election. This week has been particularly interesting for me personally because it has been a week of profound contrast.

See, on Tuesday, at the White House, we celebrated the International Day of the Girl and Let Girls Learn. (Applause.) And it was a wonderful celebration. It was the last event that I'm going to be doing as First Lady for Let Girls Learn. And I had the pleasure of spending hours talking to some of the most amazing young women you will ever meet, young girls here in the United States and all around the world. And we talked about their hopes and their dreams. We talked about their aspirations. See, because many of these girls have faced unthinkable obstacles just to attend school, jeopardizing their personal safety, their freedom, risking the rejection of their families and communities. So I thought it would be important to remind these young women how valuable and precious they are. I wanted them to understand that the measure of any society is how it treats its women and girls. (Applause.) And I told them that they deserve to be treated with dignity and respect, and I told them that they should disregard anyone who demeans or devalues them, and that they should make their voices heard in the world. And I walked away feeling so inspired, just like I'm inspired by all the young people here—(applause)—and I was so uplifted by these girls. That was Tuesday.

And now, here I am, out on the campaign trail in an election where we have consistently been hearing hurtful, hateful language about women—language that has been painful for so many of us, not just as women, but as parents trying to protect our children and raise them to be caring, respectful adults, and as citizens who think that our nation's leaders should meet basic standards of human decency. (Applause.)

The fact is that in this election, we have a candidate for President of the United States who, over the course of his lifetime and the course of this campaign, has said things about women that are so shocking, so demeaning that I simply will not repeat anything here today. And last week, we saw this candidate actually bragging about sexually assaulting women. And I can't believe that I'm saying that a candidate for President of the United States has bragged about sexually assaulting women.

And I have to tell you that I can't stop thinking about this. It has shaken me to my core in a way that I couldn't have predicted. So while I'd love nothing more than to pretend like this isn't happening, and to come out here and do my normal campaign speech, it would be dishonest and disingenuous to me to just move on to the next thing like this was all just a bad dream.

This is not something that we can ignore. It's not something we can just sweep under the rug as just another disturbing footnote in a sad election season. Because this was not just a "lewd conversation." This wasn't just locker-room banter. This was a powerful individual speaking freely and openly about sexually predatory behavior, and actually bragging about kissing and groping women, using language so obscene that many of us were worried about our children hearing it when we turn on the TV.

And to make matters worse, it now seems very clear that this isn't an isolated incident. It's one of countless examples of how he has treated women his whole life. And I have to tell you that I listen to all of this and I feel it so personally, and I'm sure that many of you do too, particularly the women. The shameful comments about our bodies. The disrespect of our ambitions and intellect. The belief that you can do anything you want to a woman.

It is cruel. It's frightening. And the truth is, it hurts. It hurts. It's like that sick, sinking feeling you get when you're walking down the street minding your own business and some guy yells out vulgar words about your body. Or when you see that guy at work that stands just a little too close, stares a little too long, and makes you feel uncomfortable in your own skin.

It's that feeling of terror and violation that too many women have felt when someone has grabbed them, or forced himself on them and they've said no but he didn't listen—something that we know happens on college campuses and countless other places every single day. It reminds us of stories we heard from our mothers and grandmothers about how, back in their day, the boss could say and do whatever he pleased to the women in the office, and even though they worked so hard, jumped over every hurdle to prove themselves, it was never enough.

We thought all of that was ancient history, didn't we? And so many have worked for so many years to end this kind of violence and abuse and disrespect, but here we are, in 2016, and we're hearing these exact same things every day on the campaign trail. We are drowning in it. And all of us are doing what women have always done: We're trying to keep our heads above water, just trying to get through it, trying to pretend like this doesn't really bother us maybe because we think that admitting how much it hurts makes us as women look weak. Maybe we're afraid to be that vulnerable. Maybe we've grown accustomed to swallowing these emotions and staying quiet, because we've seen that people often won't take our word over his. Or maybe we don't want to believe that there are still people out there who think so little of us as women. Too many are treating this as just another day's headline, as if our outrage is overblown or unwarranted, as if this is normal, just politics as usual.

But, New Hampshire, be clear: This is not normal. This is not politics as usual. (Applause.) This is disgraceful. It is intolerable. And it doesn't matter what party you belong to—Democrat, Republican, Independent—no woman deserves to be treated this way. None of us deserves this kind of abuse. (Applause.)

And I know it's a campaign, but this isn't about politics. It's about basic human decency. It's about right and wrong. (Applause.) And we simply cannot endure this, or expose our children to this any longer—not for another minute, and let alone for four years. (Applause.) Now is the time for all of us to stand up and say enough is enough. (Applause.) This has got to stop right now. (Applause.)

Because consider this: If all of this is painful to us as grown women, what do you think this is doing to our children? What message are our little girls hearing about who they should look like, how they should act? What lessons are they learning about their value as professionals, as human beings, about their dreams and aspirations? And how is this affecting men and boys in this country? Because I can tell you that the men in my life do not talk about women like this. And I know that my family is not unusual. (Applause.) And to dismiss this as everyday locker-room talk is an insult to decent men everywhere. (Applause.)

The men that you and I know don't treat women this way. They are loving fathers who are sickened by the thought of their daughters being exposed to this kind of vicious language about women. They are husbands and brothers and sons who don't tolerate women being treated and demeaned and disrespected. (Applause.) And like us, these men are worried about the impact this election is having on our boys who are looking for role models of what it means to be a man. (Applause.)

In fact, someone recently told me a story about their six-year-old son who one day was watching the news—they were watching the news together. And the little boy, out of the blue, said, "I think Hillary Clinton will be President." And his mom said, "Well, why do you say that?" And this little six-year-old said, "Because the other guy called someone a piggy, and," he said, "you cannot be President if you call someone a piggy." (Applause.)

So even a six-year-old knows better. A six-year-old knows that this is not how adults behave. This is not how decent human beings behave. And this is certainly not how someone who wants to be President of the United States behaves. (Applause.)

Because let's be very clear: Strong men—men who are truly role models—don't need to put down women to make themselves feel powerful. (Applause.) People who are truly strong lift others up. People who are truly powerful bring others together. And that is what we need in our next President. We need someone who is a uniting force in this country. We need someone who will heal the wounds that divide us, someone who truly cares about us and our children, someone with strength and compassion to lead this country forward. (Applause.)

And let me tell you, I'm here today because I believe with all of my heart that Hillary Clinton will be that President. (Applause.)

See, we know that Hillary is the right person for the job because we've seen her character and commitment not just in this campaign, but over the course of her entire life. The fact is that Hillary embodies so many of the values that we try so hard to teach our young people. We tell our young people "Work hard in school, get a good education." We encourage them to use that education to help others—which is exactly what Hillary did with her college and law degrees, advocating for kids with disabilities, fighting for children's health care as First Lady, affordable child care in the Senate. (Applause.)

We teach our kids the value of being a team player, which is what Hillary exemplified when she lost the 2008 election and actually agreed to work for her opponent as our Secretary of State—(applause)—earning sky-high approval ratings serving her country once again. (Applause.)

We also teach our kids that you don't take shortcuts in life, and you strive for meaningful success in whatever job you do. Well, Hillary has been a lawyer, a law professor, First Lady of Arkansas, First Lady of the United States, a U.S. senator, Secretary of State. And she has been successful in every role, gaining more experience and exposure to the presidency than any candidate in our lifetime—more than Barack, more than Bill. (Applause.) And, yes, she happens to be a woman. (Applause.)

And finally, we teach our kids that when you hit challenges in life, you don't give up, you stick with it. Well, during her four years as Secretary of State alone, Hillary has faced her share of challenges. She's traveled to 112 countries, negotiated a ceasefire, a peace agreement, a release of dissidents. She spent 11 hours testifying before a congressional committee. We know that when things get tough, Hillary doesn't complain. She doesn't blame others. She doesn't abandon ship for something easier. No, Hillary Clinton has never quit on anything in her life. (Applause.)

So in Hillary, we have a candidate who has dedicated her life to public service, someone who has waited her turn and helped out while waiting. (Applause.) She is an outstanding mother. She has raised a phenomenal young woman. She is a loving, loyal wife. She's a devoted daughter who cared for her mother until her final days. And if any of us had raised a daughter like Hillary Clinton, we would be so proud. We would be proud. (Applause.)

And regardless of who her opponent might be, no one could be more qualified for this job than Hillary—no one. And in this election, if we turn away from her, if we just stand by and allow her opponent to be elected, then what are we teaching our children about the values they should hold, about the kind of life they should lead? What are we saying?

In our hearts, we all know that if we let Hillary's opponent win this election, then we are sending a clear message to our kids that everything they're seeing and hearing is perfectly okay. We are validating it. We are endorsing it. We're telling our sons that it's okay to humiliate women. We're telling our daughters that this is how they deserve to be treated. We're telling all our kids that bigotry and bullying are perfectly acceptable in the leader of their country. Is that what we want for our children?

AUDIENCE: No!

MRS. OBAMA: And remember, we won't just be setting a bad example for our kids, but for our entire world. Because for so long, America has been a model for countries across the globe, pushing them to educate their girls, insisting that they give more rights to their women. But if we have a President who routinely degrades women, who brags about sexually assaulting women, then how can we maintain our moral authority in the world? How can we continue to be a beacon of freedom and justice and human dignity? (Applause.)

Well, fortunately, New Hampshire, here's the beauty: We have everything we need to stop this madness. You see, while our mothers and grandmothers were often powerless to change their circumstances, today, we as women have all the power we need to determine the outcome of this election. (Applause.)

We have knowledge. We have a voice. We have a vote. And on November the 8th, we as women, we as Americans, we as decent human beings can come together and declare that enough is enough, and we do not tolerate this kind of behavior in this country. (Applause.)

Remember this: In 2012, women's votes were the difference between Barack winning and losing in key swing states, including right here in New Hampshire. (Applause.) So for anyone who might be thinking that your one vote doesn't really matter, or that one person can't really make a difference, consider this: Back in 2012, Barack won New Hampshire by about 40,000 votes, which sounds like a lot. But when you break that number down, the difference between winning and losing this state was only 66 votes per precinct. Just take that in. If 66 people each precinct had gone the other way, Barack would have lost.

So each of you right here today could help swing an entire precinct and win this election for Hillary just by getting yourselves, your families, and your friends and neighbors out to vote. You can do it right here. (Applause.) But you could also help swing an entire precinct for Hillary's opponent with a protest vote or by staying home out of frustration.

Because here's the truth: Either Hillary Clinton or her opponent will be elected President this year. And if you vote for someone other than Hillary, or if you don't vote at all, then you are helping to elect her opponent. And just think about how you will feel if that happens. Imagine waking up on November the 9th and looking into the eyes of your daughter or son, or looking into your own eyes as you stare into the mirror. Imagine how you'll feel if you stayed home, or if you didn't do everything possible to elect Hillary.

We simply cannot let that happen. We cannot allow ourselves to be so disgusted that we just shut off the TV and walk away. And we can't just sit around wringing our hands. Now, we need to recover from our shock and depression and do what women have always done in this country. We need you to roll up your sleeves. We need to get to work. (Applause.) Because remember this: When they go low, we go —

AUDIENCE: High!

MRS. OBAMA: Yes, we do. (Applause.)

And voting ourselves is a great start, but we also have to step up and start organizing. So we need you to make calls, and knock on doors, and get folks to the polls on Election Day, and sign up to volunteer with one of the Hillary campaign folks who are here today just waiting for you to step up. (Applause.)

And, young people and not-so-young people, get on social media. (Applause.) Share your own story of why this election matters, why it should matter for all people of conscience in this country. There is so much at stake in this election.

See, the choice you make November 8th could determine whether we have a President who treats people with respect—or not. A President who will fight for kids, for good schools, for good jobs for our families—or not. A President who thinks that women deserve the right to make our own choices about our bodies and our health—or not. (Applause.) That's just a little bit of what's at stake.

So we cannot afford to be tired or turned off. And we cannot afford to stay home on Election Day. Because on November the 8th, we have the power to show our children that America's greatness comes from recognizing the innate dignity and worth of all our people. On November the 8th, we can show our children that this country is big enough to have a place for us all—men and women, folks of every background and walk of life—and that each of us is a precious part of this great American story, and we are always stronger together. (Applause.)

On November 8th, we can show our children that here in America, we reject hatred and fear—(applause)—and in difficult times, we don't discard our highest ideals. No, we rise up to meet them. We rise up to perfect our union. We rise up to defend our blessings of liberty. We rise up to embody the values of equality and opportunity and sacrifice that have always made this country the greatest nation on Earth. (Applause.)

That is who we are. (Applause.) And don't ever let anyone tell you differently. (Applause.) Hope is important. Hope is important for our young people. And we deserve a President who can see those truths in us—a President who can bring us together and bring out the very best in us. Hillary Clinton will be that President. (Applause.)

So for the next 26 days, we need to do everything we can to help her and Tim Kaine win this election. I know I'm going to be doing it. Are you with me? (Applause.) Are you all with me? (Applause.) You ready to roll up your sleeves? Get to work knocking on doors?

All right, let's get to work. Thank you all. God bless. (Applause.)

Print Citations

CMS: Obama, Michelle. "Remarks by the First Lady at a 'Hillary for America' Event in New Hampshire." Speech presented at Southern New Hampshire University, Manchester, NH, October, 2016. In *The Reference Shelf: Representative American Speeches 2015-2016*, edited by Betsy Maury, 145-51. Ipswich, MA: H.W. Wilson, 2016.

MLA: Obama, Michelle. "Remarks by the First Lady at a 'Hillary for America' Event in New Hampshire." Southern New Hampshire University. Manchester, NH. October, 2016. Presentation. *The Reference Shelf: Representative American Speeches 2015-2016*. Ed. Betsy Maury. Ipswich: H.W. Wilson, 2016. 145-51. Print.

APA: Obama, M. (2016). Remarks by the first lady at a "Hillary for America" event in New Hampshire. [Presentation]. *Speech presented at Southern New Hampshire University*. Manchester, NH. In Betsy Maury (Ed.), *The reference shelf: Representative American speeches 2015-2016* (pp. 145-151). Ipswich, MA: H.W. Wilson. (Original work published 2016)

5
A Global Perspective

British Prime Minister, David Cameron announces his resignation at No. 10 Downing street after the UK voted by 52% to 48% to leave the European Union after 43 years in an historic referendum, in London, United Kingdom on June 24, 2016.

Remarks on the Paris Agreement

By Barack Obama

In this speech, President Obama announces the signing of the Paris Agreement, one of the major achievements of his administration. The Paris Agreement is a pact within the United Nations Framework Convention on Climate Change dealing with greenhouse gases emissions mitigation, adaptation, and finance starting in the year 2020. President Obama announces here that the United States, along with China has signed the agreement, clearing the way for the agreement to take effect. The president has taken significant steps to address climate change—establishing the first-ever carbon emissions limits for power plants and new fuel economy standards for cars—and has viewed climate change as a vital foreign and domestic policy issue during his two terms as president. President Barack Obama is the 44th president of the United States, having been elected to office in 2008 and reelected in 2012. Prior to becoming president, Obama was a United States senator representing the state of Illinois from 2005 to 2008.

THE PRESIDENT: Good afternoon, everybody. Today is a historic day in the fight to protect our planet for future generations.

Ten months ago, in Paris, I said before the world that we needed a strong global agreement to reduce carbon pollution and to set the world on a low-carbon course. The result was the Paris Agreement. Last month, the United States and China—the world's two largest economies and largest emitters—formally joined that agreement together. And today, the world has officially crossed the threshold for the Paris Agreement to take effect.

Today, the world meets the moment. And if we follow through on the commitments that this agreement embodies, history may well judge it as a turning point for our planet.

Of course, it took a long time to reach this day. One of the reasons I ran for this office was to make America a leader in this mission. And over the past eight years, we've done just that. In 2009, we salvaged a chaotic climate summit in Copenhagen, establishing the principle that all nations have a role to play in combating climate change. And at home, we led by example, with historic investments in growing industries like wind and solar that created a steady stream of new jobs. We set the first-ever nationwide standards to limit the amount of carbon pollution that power plants can dump into the air our children breathe. From the cars and trucks we

Delivered on October 5, 2016 in Washington, DC

drive to the homes and businesses in which we live and work, we've changed fundamentally the way we consume energy.

Now, keep in mind, the skeptics said these actions would kill jobs. And instead, we saw—even as we were bringing down these carbon levels—the longest streak of job creation in American history. We drove economic output to new highs. And we drove our carbon pollution to its lowest levels in two decades.

We continued to lead by example with our historic joint announcement with China two years ago, where we put forward even more ambitious climate targets. And that achievement encouraged dozens of other countries to set more ambitious climate targets of their own. And that, in turn, paved the way for our success in Paris—the idea that no nation, not even one as powerful as ours, can solve this challenge alone. All of us have to solve it together.

Now, the Paris Agreement alone will not solve the climate crisis. Even if we meet every target embodied in the agreement, we'll only get to part of where we need to go. But make no mistake, this agreement will help delay or avoid some of the worst consequences of climate change. It will help other nations ratchet down their dangerous carbon emissions over time, and set bolder targets as technology advances, all under a strong system of transparency that allows each nation to evaluate the progress of all other nations. And by sending a signal that this is going to be our future—a clean energy future—it opens up the floodgates for businesses, and scientists, and engineers to unleash high-tech, low-carbon investment and innovation at a scale that we've never seen before. So this gives us the best possible shot to save the one planet we've got.

I know diplomacy isn't always easy, and progress on the world stage can sometimes be slow. But together, with steady persistent effort, with strong, principled, American leadership, with optimism and faith and hope, we're proving that it is possible.

And I want to embarrass my Senior Advisor, Brian Deese—who is standing right over there—because he worked tirelessly to make this deal possible. He, and John Kerry, Gina McCarthy at the EPA, everybody on their teams have done an extraordinary job to get us to this point—and America should be as proud of them as I am of them.

I also want to thank the people of every nation that has moved quickly to bring the Paris Agreement into force. I encourage folks who have not yet submitted their documentation to enter into this agreement to do so as soon as possible. And in the coming days, let's help finish additional agreements to limit aviation emissions, to phase down dangerous use of hydrofluorocarbons—all of which will help build a world that is safer, and more prosperous, and more secure, and more free than the one that was left for us.

That's our most important mission, to make sure our kids and our grandkids have at least as beautiful a planet, and hopefully more beautiful, than the one that we have. And today, I'm a little more confident that we can get the job done.

So thank you very much, everybody.

Print Citations

CMS: Obama, Barack. "Remarks on the Paris Agreement." Washington, DC, October, 2016. In *The Reference Shelf: Representative American Speeches 2015-2016*, edited by Betsy Maury, 155-57. Ipswich, MA: H.W. Wilson, 2016.

MLA: Obama, Barack. "Remarks on the Paris Agreement." Washington, DC. Presentation. October, 2016. *The Reference Shelf: Representative American Speeches 2015-2016*. Ed. Betsy Maury. Ipswich: H.W. Wilson, 2016. 155-57. Print.

APA: Obama, B. (2016). Remarks on the Paris Agreement. [Presentation]. Washington, DC. In Betsy Maury (Ed.), *The reference shelf: Representative American speeches 2015-2016* (pp. 155-157). Ipswich, MA: H.W. Wilson. (Original work published 2016)

"World 'Must Not Let Fears Get the Better of Us'"

By Angelina Jolie

In this speech delivered in the Bekaa Valley of Lebanon, Angelina Jolie, in her capacity as special envoy for United Nations High Commissioner for Refugees (UNHCR) speaks to the world about the need for political will and leadership in solving the humanitarian crisis created by the war in Syria. The refugee crisis in Europe and around the Middle East reached peak levels in 2016, with nations struggling to handle the influx of displaced people. Jolie calls on nations to make a place for these vulnerable people in their communities and calls on leaders to work together for diplomatic solutions to the world's problems. Angelina Jolie is an actress, filmmaker, and humanitarian. She is a special envoy for the UNHCR.

Good morning, I am pleased to be back in Lebanon today.

I want to thank the Lebanese people for helping to save the lives of over 1 million Syrians. It is not easy for a country to take in the equivalent of a quarter of its own population in refugees.

But for as much as it is a responsibility, I hope you are aware of the message it sends about the values and character and spirit of the Lebanese people.

You are setting an example to the world of generosity, humanity, resilience and solidarity. On behalf of UNHCR, and on my own behalf, shukran, thank you.

We should never forget that for all the focus on the refugee situation in Europe at this time, the greatest pressure is still being felt in the Middle East and North Africa, as it has for each of the last five years.

There are 4.8 million Syrian refugees in this region, and 6.5 million people displaced inside Syria. On this day, the 5th anniversary of the Syria conflict, that is where I had hoped I would be: in Syria, helping UNHCR with returns, and watching families I have come to know be able to go home.

It is tragic and shameful that we seem to be so far from that point.

Every Syrian refugee I have spoken to on this visit, without exception, talked of their desire to return home when the war is over and it is safe for them to do so—not with

---

Delivered on March 15, 2016, in the Bekaa Valley in Lebanon.

resignation, but with the light in their eyes of people dreaming of being reunited with the country that they love.

I have seen on this visit just how desperate the struggle to survive now is for these families. After five years of exile, any savings they had, have been exhausted. Many who started out living in apartments now cluster in abandoned shopping centers, or informal tented settlements, sinking deeper into debt.

The number of refugees in Lebanon living below the minimum threshold for survival unable to afford the food and shelter they need to stay alive—has doubled in the last two years, in a country where 79 percent of all Syrian refugees are women and children.

We have to understand the fundamental realities that are driving the global refugee crisis—which is the product not just of the Syria war, but of decades of open-ended conflicts or persecution: in Myanmar, Mali, the Central African Republic, the DRC, Nigeria, Somalia, South Sudan, Afghanistan, Yemen, Iraq, Syria. I could go on.

The number of refugees is now higher than the last time we had a World War. We are at an exceptionally difficult moment internationally, when the consequences of the refugee crisis seem to be outstripping our will and capacity and even our courage to respond to it.

In conventional times of war, people who are displaced go to more stable areas, or to neighboring countries for sanctuary, or are provided for in refugee camps until it is safe to go home. In exceptional circumstances some are sent abroad for resettlement or asylum.

But with 60 million people displaced, as there are today, there is no way that the governments of the world– no matter how rich or willing they are—can prop up the UN enough to care for all these people permanently and expect that to address the problem.

We cannot manage the world through aid relief in the place of diplomacy and political solutions. We cannot discuss this as if it were a problem confined to the situation of tens of thousands of refugees in Europe. We cannot improve this reality by partial responses, by responding to some crises and not others, or by helping some refugees and not others—for instance, by excluding Afghan refugees, among other groups—or by making a distinction between refugees on [the] grounds of religion. The result would be more chaos, more injustice and insecurity, and ultimately more conflict, and more refugees.

We have to focus on the absolute root causes, and that takes a certain amount of courage and leadership. And in my view, leadership in this situation is about doing more than simply protecting your borders or simply putting forward more aid, it means taking decisions to ensure we are not heading towards an even greater refugee crisis in the future.

That is why, as heartbreaking and angering it is to hear the individual stories of the refugees, it is not a time for emotion. It is a time for reason and calm and foresight.

I want to be clear that I understand that people in many different countries have fears about the refugee situation.

They are worried about the impact on their communities, livelihoods and security if they accept refugees into their countries. It is not wrong to feel unsettled face by a crisis of such complexity and such magnitude. But we must not let fears get the better of us.

We must not let fear stand in the way of an effective response that is in our long-term interests.

My plea today is that we need governments around the world to show leadership: to analyze the situation and understand exactly what their country can do, how many refugees they can assist and how, in which particular communities and to what timeframe; to explain this to their citizens and address fears—based not on emotion but on a measured assessment of what can and must be done to share the responsibility and get on top of this situation.

That starts with having a very robust asylum procedure to be able to hear the needs of the desperate families to identify who is most vulnerable and who has a genuine refugee claim—processes that UNHCR has been supporting governments to carry out for decades.

I appeal to all governments to uphold the UN Convention on Refugees and basic human rights law, because it is both necessary and possible to protect people fleeing persecution and death and protect citizens at home. It should not be reduced to a choice between one or the other.

The reason we have laws and binding international agreements is precisely because of the temptation to deviate from them in times of pressure. We know from recent history that when we depart from fundamental laws and principles we only create worse problems for the future.

I spent time this morning with a mother who was paralyzed after being shot by a sniper's rifle in a besieged area of Syria. She lies in one room, where she lives with her whole family, in a small, cold, makeshift settlement here in the Bekaa Valley. Never once during our discussion did she ask for anything, did she stop smiling, or talk of anything other than her desire for her children to have the chance to go to school and have a better life.

When I saw her beautiful smile, and her dedicated husband and children looking after her, I was in awe of them. They are heroes to me. And I ask myself, what have we come to when such survivors are made to feel like beggars?

We can do the right thing by refugees and build a more secure international environment. We can build order out of chaos.

In my view it comes down to understanding the law, choosing not to be afraid, and showing political will. For the sake of the people of Syria, and for all the refugees around the world looking desperately to the international community to provide solutions, I hope we will do this.

And I also hope that the 15th of March next year will finally herald a Syria at peace, and will be the beginning of a time of returns so that these refugees are able to fulfill their desire to go home.

Print Citations

CMS: Jolie, Angelina. "World 'Must Not Let Fears Get the Better of Us.'" Bekaa Valley, Lebanon, March, 2016. In *The Reference Shelf: Representative American Speeches 2015-2016*, edited by Betsy Maury, 158-61. Ipswich, MA: H.W. Wilson, 2016.

MLA: Jolie, Angelina. "World 'Must Not Let Fears Get the Better of Us.'" Bekaa, Lebanon. March, 2016. Presentation. *The Reference Shelf: Representative American Speeches 2015-2016*. Ed. Betsy Maury. Ipswich: H.W. Wilson, 2016. 158-61. Print.

APA: Jolie, A. (2016). World "Must not let fears get the better of us." [Presentation]. Bekaa, Lebanon. In Betsy Maury (Ed.), *The reference shelf: Representative American speeches 2015-2016* (pp. 158-161). Ipswich, MA: H.W. Wilson. (Original work published 2016)

Remarks at the Aspen Ideas Festival

By John Kerry

In this speech at the Aspen Ideas Festival, Secretary of State John Kerry informs the audience about his work around the globe. Shortly after the surprise Brexit vote in June 2016, in which the United Kingdom voted to exit the European Union, Kerry allays fears about the US ongoing engagement in Europe by saying, "And the Brexit vote in my judgment, and I think President Obama's judgment, does not affect the agenda that we share with NATO, the G7, the P5, all—and by the way, the NATO leaders." Kerry further emphasizes that the United States is "more engaged in more places with greater impact today than at any time in America's history. And that is simply documentable and undeniable." John Kerry is the 68th and current United States secretary of state. He previously served in the United States Senate representing the state of Massachusetts and is a decorated naval veteran.

SECRETARY KERRY: Thank you very much. Thank you. Well, good afternoon. Thank you. Well, let me start by apologizing for bringing you into the tent from the outside. I think that's—(laughter)—a sin against nature and instinct.

Good afternoon to all of you. Walter, what—you're disappearing—thank you. Thank you for your warm introduction. Thank you especially for your leadership role here at the Aspen Institute. And I am delighted to be back in Colorado, where I was born about 25 or 35 years ago. (Laughter.) It still feels that way, actually—(laughter)—which is good. Frankly, I am at a bit of a disadvantage compared to all of you, because I had to get up early and fly here from Washington having done a four-country visit yesterday and instead of partaking in morning yoga. (Laughter.) So what can I say? Life is real hard. (Laughter.)

In fact, I began yesterday morning in Rome with Bibi Netanyahu, where we met; and then I flew to Brussels, where I met with President Juncker and with EU High Representative Mogherini; then to London in the afternoon, where I met with my counterpart, Foreign Secretary Philip Hammond, and then with Prime Minister Cameron. And then back here—back to Washington, obviously, and now here I am, and I, as Walter said, go on to our important North American Leaders Summit tomorrow in Ottawa.

But I want to just share with you, that genuinely, coming to an ideas festival is a treat for me. And I hope we actually could share some ideas and have a little give-and-take here, which is what is refreshing and timely, and I think that's why you

Delivered on June 28, 2016, at the Aspen Institute in Aspen, Colorado.

come here, and that's what makes this valuable. After arriving here, I want you to know that I haven't thought once about the alleged scientific evidence that a whole lot of flying shrinks your brain. (Laughter.) Some of you may be saying to yourselves, "Well, that would explain a lot." (Laughter.) But I only mention it to establish a very plausible line of defense for when we get the Q&A going. (Laughter.)

You have an extraordinary syllabus here, I was looking at it—from Obama's foreign policy—I think it's The World According to Obama, the World According to Star Wars (inaudible), Ripple and Einstein's Legacy, Mandarin in 60 Minutes—(laughter)—Futuristic Farming—I mean, you read the list, it's pretty extraordinary, and that's what makes this event both so stimulating and so much fun. But needless to say, I intend to be a little more prosaic and I hope not pedantic and talk to you about the world as I see it from my vantage point as Secretary of State, which I've been privileged to do now for three and a half years.

Now, unless you all spent the entire week hiking and sleeping without your cell phone—which is very enticing, believe me—(laughter)—you have undoubtedly been reading, thinking, and talking about Brexit, and maybe in the Q&A we'll talk about it in a little bit. I mentioned I talked to the leaders from the UK, EU—I left out NATO. I met also with Jens Stoltenberg. And my message to all of them was very simple—that America's commitment to the EU and to Great Britain is as strong as ever to both the transatlantic partnership and to our special relationship. And the Brexit vote in my judgment, and I think President Obama's judgment, does not affect the agenda that we share with NATO, the G7, the P5, all—and by the way, the NATO leaders, we will all be meeting in about a week in Warsaw for the NATO summit, and it actually makes that summit more important and it makes much of what we will be doing to reassure the front-line states and to make it clear how important that alliance still remains. So we will continue to collaborate with both the British and the EU.

And I want to just emphasize, as I did in England yesterday, the values that we have shared for so long with our friends, the Brits, and that we shared in the vision of an EU, and the interests and its interests and values that make up foreign policy and its interests and values that brought us together—they are the same today as they were before the vote last Wednesday. Didn't change a thing. So remember that as we go forward, and I reminded both parties how critical it is to remain steady here. And the steadiness of our purpose, I think, is evident and embraced by all, and the ability to rely on capable partners right now in this world that we're living in is more critical than ever, because it is increasingly clear that pundits and practitioners alike understand more and more of how we are living in a much more complex world than at any time in our history.

For years, if you go back to the fall of the Berlin Wall and the great changes that came about thereafter—Tito, Yugoslavia—I mean, societies were compressed by the Cold War, by the entire post-World War II order. And a lot of societies were shielded by the absence of communication, by the slow pace of doing business if they did business at all effectively, and by the simplicity of the bipolar East-West divide which defined the world for the latter part and even for most of since 1917—for most of the 20th century.

Now, as every single one of you knows and as you talk about in every which way as we contemplate various disruptors in our lives and in society, we are dealing with a world which speeds up politics, speeds up the flow of information beyond the capacity of most people to digest it. And believe me, that was underscored by the fact that I noticed that the largest Internet Google search in England the day after the vote was "What is the EU?" (Laughter.) I'm serious.

So this is a world where globalization and instantaneous communication are connecting people in more ways than ever before. The kids in Tahrir Square—that wasn't motivated by any religious extremism, nor were the kids who originally came out in Syria to demonstrate for a future. The fact is that we see more people connected in more ways than ever before, and so everybody knows what everybody else has, and that underscores what you don't have. It facilitates both incredible technological progress, but—and obviously economic growth that goes with it. I was just in Silicon Valley last week with the various CEOs of major companies there, listening to this discussion about these disruptors, which is fascinating. Any of you in the retail business understand what I'm talking about.

But at the same time, there are a whole bunch of folks who believe they've been left behind. And in many places, my friends, they have been. And they're increasingly turning to a narrow-minded tribalism, to aggressive nationalism, and even medieval thinking that reminds us of a very distant and bloody past.

So we have no illusion—I certainly have no illusion—about the challenges. They are real in this 21st century. And while there are a lot of Cassandras around, I really don't believe the road ahead is defined only by turmoil and strife.

After all, it really wasn't long ago that we saw a rapidly expanding nuclear program in Iran, only months away from having enough weapons-grade uranium to build 10 to 12 nuclear weapons, and we were on the cusp of confrontation. Now, because of the Joint Comprehensive Plan of Action, Iran's path to actually building a bomb has been closed off—and I say "closed off" because you can't build a bomb with 3.67 percent limit on enrichment and with 300 kilograms of a stockpile. You just can't do it physically. And because we have 130 additional inspectors and all kinds of different ways in which we will know what is going on.

By taking away the potential of a nuclear weapon in a country that we still have other issues with—nobody pretends they've been erased—we have changed the strategic equation.

Last December, representatives from more than 190 nations came together in Paris to express their commitment to build a new low-carbon energy future for the world in which greenhouse gas emissions are curbed and the worst consequences of climate change are prevented.

Last October, after seven years of negotiation, the United States joined 11 other nations along the Pacific Rim in signing and sending to the Congress the Trans-Pacific Partnership, a trade agreement unlike any trade agreement we've had before. And I, 28 years in the Senate, voted for all the trade agreements. But this is unlike any of those I voted for because within the four corners of the agreement, there are labor standards, there are environment standards, and it encompasses nearly 40 percent of global GDP. It's a game-changer.

Last August, I had the privilege of traveling to Havana to raise the American flag above our embassy for the first time in 54 years—a change of a policy that has already had a profound impact in the world. (Applause.)

And together with a broad array of partners around the world, we have mobilized a coalition to stop the spread of Ebola and save countless lives. And remember, last year the predictions were by Christmastime a million people were going to die. But President Obama had the courage to send 3,000 American troops, and they had the courage to go and be part of this effort, and we stopped it together with Great Britain and France and the help of other nations around the world.

Through PEPFAR and other efforts, we now stand on the brink of the first AIDS-free generation. (Applause.)

So ladies and gentlemen—(applause)—so I just say this to underscore to you that the world is not witnessing global gridlock. We are not frozen in a nightmare. And the facts and the lessons are clear that where we are engaged with a clear strategy and where we use our power thoughtfully, we are making progress in most places. I'm not going to pretend everywhere, and I'll talk about where we aren't. But nobody said things would be easy or that we would all get it done all at once. What I find exciting about this moment is that we are staring at extraordinary opportunities everywhere if we look and make the right choices.

So don't forget—a lot of people do—our boldest predecessors overcame depression, fascism, two world wars by singularly focusing on the challenge at hand. But today, as I've described, we face multiple overriding challenges of varying origin that require varying approaches all at the same time. And we're working with countries now—and just as an example, we are deeply enmeshed, we have a special envoy that we appointed to work with the Government of Colombia to try to achieve a just and lasting peace, a signing just a week or two ago—a few days ago. We hope to have that finished within a matter of a month or two. We've been working with countries to support a new Government of National Accord in Libya. I was recently in the United Arab Emirates. I think we've come to a common understanding of how to strengthen that government and go after Daesh in Libya. We're supporting Afghanistan in its fight against extremists and support a sovereign and democratic Ukraine. And so that is why I state unabashedly to every single one of you: the United States of America is more engaged in more places with greater impact today than at any time in America's history. And that is simply documentable and undeniable. (Applause.)

Now, this is an ideas festival, and I want to talk to you about what I see after years of being involved in public life and about the problems we face, because I am convinced there are three particular challenges, each of which requires that we show that singularity of purpose and focus that our parents and grandparents did in the course of the last century. And that is to have a intense shared focus.

The first is violent extremism and the emergence of radical non-state actors, as opposed to state actors, which defined the last century for the most part.

I might just comment—I want to make sure publicly that I comment that just today, a bomb went off at the airport in Istanbul. Ten people we know are—according to the press reports, at least—are dead and some 40 wounded, and we are still collecting information and trying to ascertain what happened and who did it. And I won't comment further on it, except to say that this is daily fare. And that's why I say the first challenge we need to face is countering non-state violent actors, for a host of reasons.

The second is the need, more urgent than ever and more urgent, certainly, than some national politicians seem willing to admit, to preserve the health of our planet in the face of imminent climate change—happening climate change—and other environmental dangers.

And the third is connected to the other two, and it's part and parcel of how we're going to solve the whole problem. It is a global crisis of governance that will require leaders everywhere to cooperate, fight corruption, earn public confidence, inspire unity, and actually make decisions about issues that are relevant to the people who populate our countries.

Now, I hope in the Q&A we'll talk a little more about the climate and the governance, because they're worth some focus. But let me focus for the moment just in these comments—and then we'll get into Q&A—about the struggle against violent extremism.

Everybody knows the threat. We've all awakened to the news that I just announced to you. How many times have you awakened to it? Vicious attacks perpetrated by a lone wolf or by a group, inspired on the Internet or otherwise. From Orlando to San Bernardino to the Philippines and Bali, we've seen pictures and we've heard testimony of shocking crimes committed by al-Qaida, by Boko Haram, by Jaysh al-Islam, by Ahrar al-Sham, by al-Shabaab, Daesh, other groups against innocent civilians, against journalists, and against teachers particularly. And we're all aware that Daesh uses sexual slavery as a recruitment tool, and it pins price tags on little girls to help finance its operations. This is the reward of going to fight. And we've heard Daesh's preposterous boast to be the creator of a new caliphate and the leader of all Islam.

So two summers ago, when Daesh began its rampage in Iraq, please remember, we heard dire predictions of a permanent unraveling in the Middle East, the erasure of national boundaries, the prospect that Baghdad itself might fall and come under the sway of the terrorists. At a time when Daesh and its black flags and its 50-caliber mounted Toyotas were careening through Syria and Iraq, people thought Baghdad might fall. President Obama immediately mobilized our air power and we moved to save thousands of people at Sinjar Mountain who were about to be slaughtered by Daesh. Then the President directed me to go about and build a coalition which is now at 66 members with representatives from across the globe. And we will all be meeting together in Washington in a few weeks, July 21st, to measure our progress.

So at this festival of ideas, my idea is, frankly, pretty straightforward: We have to complete the job. We have to defeat Daesh, its affiliates, and its imitators in Afghanistan, Libya, Nigeria, elsewhere—wherever they raise their ugly head. And that is not an option my friends, that is an imperative. It is critical to our national security because we know they're plotting and we know what they will do to other countries in the region who are our allies and friends and important to the stability of the world. And make no mistake; this is not a clash of civilizations, this is a clash of civilization against a kind of barbarism—between civilization and medieval and modern fascism wrapped together at the same time and, yes, between a cultural clash with modernity and the failure of governments to do anything for some of these countries over the last 50 years or more. So it will take years of determined effort, but the effort has to be determined. And it'll take sacrifice to succeed. But think back to what I said about the last century and sacrifice.

The good news is we have absolutely, certainly, without any doubt whatsoever started down the right path. Last year at this time in the core areas of Iraq and Syria we were containing the terrorists of Daesh. Now we are moving methodically and authoritatively to destroy them, to take back territory, and put Daesh on the final path to defeat.

To date, our coalition has conducted some 38,00 airstrikes, we've taken out more than 120 known, identifiable high-level leaders, and we have caused the ranks of Daesh to shrink by one-third.

Together with our partners, we have pushed Daesh out of nearly half of the populated territory it once controlled in Iraq and about a quarter of the land that it controlled and occupied in Syria. And I am currently involved in discussions with the Russians now to see if we can change the structure of this current ceasefire and actually make progress with respect to taking out all of the terrorists in the country while also trying to find a political solution to the challenge. We have liberated Tikrit, Sinjar, Ramadi, Hasakah, and Kobani. And Iraqi Security Forces have just taken back the key city of Fallujah. And local forces in Syria are pressing Daesh in the strategic town of Manbij.

And now we understand much better how Daesh operates. We are enabled to adjust our targeting; more effectively hammer its heavy weapons, its training camps, supply routes, its infrastructure. We have destroyed over 400 of its tanker trucks that were taking oil out to Turkey or Iraq in order to sell it and fund their operations. We have cut their revenue at least in half, and without additional towns to plunder, Daesh has less money to buy weapons or pay its fighters. We're also working diligently to destroy Daesh's narrative—the narrative that they are successful, that they hold territory, they are a state, that they are the caliphate of the future. All of that narrative is what has drawn fighters from France, from Germany, from the United States, from Australia, from around the world. And we are working diligently on a whole counter-narrative strategy together with our friends in the Middle East and elsewhere. So it has been more than one year since Daesh has actually launched a full-scale military offensive, and that's because our coalition is moving forward relentlessly on every front.

Now, yes, you can bomb an airport. You can blow yourself up. That's the tragedy. Daesh and others like it know that we have to get it right 24/7/365. They have to get it right for 10 minutes or one hour. So it's a very different scale. And if you're desperate and if you know you're losing and you know you want to give up your life, then obviously you can do some harm.

So our fight from Daesh in Iraq and Syria is not over. The big tests are still ahead, especially in retaking Mosul, which is the largest remaining stronghold in Iraq, though we have now surrounded it and we are laying the groundwork for an offensive; and, of course, al-Raqqa in Syria.

Let me be blunt: Taking out Daesh is only one part of this struggle. We have to, as a nation, and particularly a Congress and an Executive, come together to engage in a far more comprehensive effort against the forces that make terrorism a global, not just a regional, threat. To confront this challenge I recently created the first Countering Violent Extremism Office in the State Department and I introduced a new strategy together with President Obama, a new strategy at the White House pursuing—all joined together—and our Defense Department—in order to have one united front to counter this violent extremism.

But listen to the words of Henry David Thoreau—a long time ago he got it right: "There are a thousand hacking at the branches of evil, to only one who is striking at the root." Clearly, we have to strike relentlessly at the root causes of violent extremism or we're going to play extremist whack-a-mole for years to come. And we can't do that unless we first understand those roots.

After serving in public life now for over three decades I am aware that there are few more reliable and easy punchlines on the stump when you're running for office than to stand up and promise to slash the budget of the State Department or USAID and just say very simply, we shouldn't be spending money over there on those people, we need to spend it right here in good old Iowa, Indiana, Illinois, wherever the hell it is, and everybody erupts into applause. That makes sense. Easiest thing in the world. Good applause line; lousy policy—shortsighted, self-inflictive of harm to our own nation.

I know in Washington, particularly the Washington of today, that long-term goals can sometimes get really quickly wiped out by visible short-term projects or just short-term responses. But that's exactly why we need to take the long view and we need to recognize how relatively modest investments now can improve the world enormously and enhance our security for generations to come.

My friends, we are the richest economy on the face of this planet—$18 trillion economy. We spend one penny of every single dollar that we spend, on all of our foreign aid initiatives, all of our State Department, all of our embassies, everything we do for diplomacy. One penny on the dollar. The richest economy in the world cannot be content to put one penny on the dollar into the effort to protect our nation.

And as we've learned in this era, poisonous ideas can come from many places—an inflammatory sermon, a radical teacher, an angry parent, a woman on a website, or a man in the next cell. They might originate with pictures seen on the nightly news, or from perceived acts of discrimination or repression, or from the desire to avenge the death of a loved one. They might grow out of illness, envy, desperation, or a personal craving for fame at the cost of self-destruction.

So here's the question—how do we help give young people here and across the globe something better to hold on to? The full answer to that, obviously, would require a whole shelf of books, not brief remarks, but the chapter headings might include the following.

First, fight corruption—because there is a direct link between corruption and the rise of violent extremism. Nothing does more to undermine respect for the rule of law than the perception that governments consider themselves to be above the law. How astonishing it is that billions of dollars were stolen—maybe $50 billion from the Government of Nigeria, maybe $30 billion from the Government of Yemen—and that is stealing from the education and the health and the infrastructure and the future of the citizens of those countries. And what about the banks that deposit that money and second it for those who have stolen it? It's little wonder that there is great unrest in certain parts of the world. And if we're serious about fighting terrorism, then we have to expose corruption, and protect whistleblowers, and prosecute perpetrators, and throw the guilty in jail. And at the same time, we have to strive for improved governance across the board. What does that mean? That means preventing graft, strengthening democratic and accountable governance, where basic freedoms are protected and people have the ability to express their views openly, without harassment, and without fear. After all, if citizens are going to respect their governments, then governments need to respect their citizens.

Now, second, we have to invest in education. I can't emphasize this enough. Globally, right now—(applause)—right now as we sit here in Aspen, in these extraordinary surroundings, 120 million children and adolescents are out of school. We can't settle for a policy, my friends, that plans to get these kids in school in 10 years. You're 10 years old today, nine years old, seven years old—you're going to be 17, 18 before somebody starts to teach you something? They need to go to school now. And we need an emergency global education effort. When I was in Pakistan as a senator, I went up to the area of the earthquake you remember a few years ago, up near the mountains of the Himalayas, and I remember these kids would come down out of the mountains, and they were in a tent with desks and a chair, and they had uniforms somehow that someone had gotten them. And half of these kids were in school for the first time in their life. And why were they there? They were there because of an emergency that brought them there.

Well, I'm telling you I don't think we should wait for a flood or an earthquake. We have an emergency now and we should treat this as if it were an emergency now, and make sure these kids are getting the education that they need.

Now, terrorist recruiters are on the prowl—(applause)—if I were running for office, I'd milk that; I'd—(laughter)—try to—but I'm not. I'm sorry. (Laughter and applause.) Terrorist recruiters are literally prowling around. I have a foreign—I won't tell you which country, but in Africa, my counterpart told me how you grab these kids at age five, and they pay them, and then they proselytize, then they don't need to proselytize because their minds are gone, and they've got them, and then they don't have to pay them. Then they go out and get the next group. And my counterpart, the foreign minister of this country, said to me, "You know, they have a plan for 30 years or 35 years; we don't even have a five-year plan."

So think about it. To win the battle of ideas, we have to ensure that kids everywhere actually have schools to go to, that schools don't preach hate and radical views, but they offer an opportunity to prepare for a better life. And guess what? That does take a little bit of money. Not as much as people think, but I am convinced when you think of the other side on which we wind up paying for all of this, it is far cheaper to do it up front and far more effective in so many different ways.

Third thing we need to do is close the gap between what students learn in class and the skills that they'll need in the workplace, in today's workplace. And that means addressing unequal access to unemployment and promoting lifelong learning and on-the-job training, not just in other countries, but also right here at home, above all. (Applause.) And we need to—we have an effort called Global Connect which we've started, because we're trying to connect the other 60 percent of the people in the world who do not have the Internet yet and need it.

Fourth, we have to give entrepreneurs and small business people everywhere the chance to translate their good new ideas into thriving businesses, because innovation is by far, as I'm sure all of you here know, the primary source of job creation. And that means ending the suffocating stranglehold in some countries of militaries and bureaucracies that suck up the private sector to the detriment of the rest of the citizens in the country or the rest of the legitimate business people. It means opening doors to the full participation by women. And there's literally no way we are going to meet the 21st century expectations with 20th century economic policies or 19th century standards of governance.

Finally, we need to draw the basic ideas that have guided America for centuries. I don't know about you, I am obsessed by *Hamilton* and I keep listening to it. It's magnificent—(laughter and applause)—and it reminds us about those ideas.

And if we are consistent in showing the world what we are for, we will never lack allies in the fight against bigotry and terror.

And the reason for that is clear. A group like Daesh—in fact, all of these groups: Boko Haram, al-Shabaab, all of them, they're all the same in this regard—they don't have any room for anyone else, folks. If they're allowed to prevail it would utterly destroy the human mosaic that has existed in the Middle East for countless generations. It castigates—Daesh castigates Yezidis as devil worshippers. It tells Christians, quote, "We will conquer your Rome, break your crosses, and enslave your women." It says of Shia Muslims, quote, "We have a duty to kill them, fight them, displace them, and cleanse the land of their filth."

Obviously, you're here celebrating the best of our country, which is a festival of ideas, where we have every opportunity to share our opinions, discuss alternative policies, explain respectfully why those with whom we disagree are mistaken.

And one of the things I've learned after years of public life is there are no end to the tests for our country. The testing is constant. But compared to 1950, when the Aspen Institute was founded, we have tremendous advantages. Since then, through American leadership and the combined efforts of good people across the globe, average life expectancy is up 50 percent. Infant mortality is down by four-fifths. The number of democracies has nearly quadrupled. The rate of extreme poverty has just this year fallen below 10 percent for the first time ever. Overall, a child entering the world today is more likely than ever before in history to be born healthy, to have vaccinations, to be adequately fed, to be able to get the necessary education, and more likely to live a long life.

So I think we have every reason to be confident in the future, provided we are willing to make the investments that leaders have a responsibility to make, provided we do not allow the passions of the day to turn our heads and leave us fighting with one another, and provided we draw the right lessons from our own past. We also need to believe in basic facts and science.

Sixty-eight years ago—(applause)—I'll close just by sharing with you that 68 years ago this week, the United States and its allies launched Operation Vittles in response to the Soviet blockade of ground routes into the encircled city of West Berlin. If we had done nothing, the city would have fallen into communist hands. But the alternative—supplying 2.5 million people entirely by air, using the very small, slow planes of the era—seemed daunting or impossible. Nothing like it had ever been done before, but Harry Truman made the bold decision that we were going to do it—to do it anyway.

The allied pilots were not only American; they were Australian, British, Canadian, French, New Zealanders, South African. And imagine their planes like a long line of birds lined up across the heavens from one end to the other, flying 1,398 missions on a single day—their cargo holds piled full of food, medicine, and coal. The Soviets sought desperately to jam the communications, but ultimately, after 320 days of continuous airlifts, they gave in. The crisis was over. The city was saved.

Today, we have to act with similar resolve. We have to come to the aid of countries that are on the front lines or the next in lines of the targets of terrorist infiltration.

We have to improve governance, fight corruption, promote accountability, respect human rights. We have to teach the skills and create the jobs that will make extremist appeals fall on deaf ears. And we have to innovate and build as if our entire generation and the next generation depend on it. Because, guess what? They do. And we have to maintain relentless pressure on Daesh and its allies until they are thoroughly defeated, both on the field of battle and in the minds of people everywhere.

For these not just to be words, these things I've talked about, we need to get all the institutions of our government pulling together. And above all, we need to protect the security of our country, and as the leader of the free world, live up to our own leadership expectations. Nothing will speak to the current unease more than getting the things done that need to be done. And I promise you that right up until the last day, President Obama and I intend to put our full commitment into doing exactly that.

Thank you all very, very much. (Applause.) Thank you. Thank you very much.

Print Citations

CMS: Kerry, John. "Remarks at the Aspen Ideas Festival." Speech presented at the Aspen Institute, Aspen, CO, June, 2016. In *The Reference Shelf: Representative American Speeches 2015-2016*, edited by Betsy Maury, 162-72. Ipswich, MA: H.W. Wilson, 2016.

MLA: Kerry, John. "Remarks at the Aspen Ideas Festival." Aspen Institute. Aspen, CO. June, 2016. Presentation. *The Reference Shelf: Representative American Speeches 2015-2016*. Ed. Betsy Maury. Ipswich: H.W. Wilson, 2016. 162-72. Print.

APA: Kerry, J. (2016). Remarks at the Aspen ideas festival. [Presentation]. *Speech presented at the Aspen Institute*. Aspen, CO. In Betsy Maury (Ed.), *The reference shelf: Representative American speeches 2015-2016* (pp. 162-172). Ipswich, MA: H.W. Wilson. (Original work published 2016)

Keynote Speech at
World Humanitarian Day

By Chimamanda Ngozi Adichie

In this keynote address at the United Nations, Nigerian novelist Chimamanda Ngozi Adichie speaks about her own parents' experiences as refugees during the Biafra War and calls on listeners to find some understanding for refugees, who are in need of not only food and shelter but dignity and love. She calls on nations to live up to obligations to refugees and calls on people to make room for people in need. Chimamanda Ngozi Adichie is a Nigerian novelist, nonfiction and short story writer.

Distinguished guests, ladies and gentlemen, good evening. I'm very honored to be here.

In 1967, almost 50 years ago, my parents lived in Nsukka, a university town in Eastern Nigeria. They had 2 small children, a house, a car, friends. A stable life. Then the Nigeria Biafra War started.

Only days later, my parents heard the sound of shelling and gunfire. So frightening, so close, that they had very little time to pack anything before they ran. They left almost all their belongings behind.

They ended up in another town, a town already very crowded. They could not find a place to stay. Even the refugee camps were full. My father was desperate. He was worried about being out in the open, because of the possibility of air raids. He knew a man who was from that town, a man named Emmanuel Isike. Emmanuel lived in a cramped house, that was full of people. Members of his extended family, people whose homes the war had also smashed.

My father also knew that it would be very difficult for Emmanuel to accommodate them. Very difficult to stretch what was already badly stretched. Still, my father knocked on Emmanuel's door. Emmanuel looked at my parents, holding on to their 2 small daughters, their faces shadowed in despair. And he said, "We will make room for you." I think often of that moment. Because I wonder if my parents would've survived the war, had they not benefited from that act of kindness?

For 3 years, my parents were refugees. And they owed a lot, not only to Emmanuel, but also to many humanitarian workers. Those women and men, magnificent in their bravery and their vulnerability and their commitment. But my parents were

---

Delivered on August 19, 2016, at the World Humanitarian Day event in New York, New York.

not just refugees. Nobody is ever just a refugee. Nobody is ever just a single thing. And yet, in the public discourse today, we often speak of people as single things. Refugee, immigrant. We dehumanize people when we reduce them to a single thing. And this dehumanization is insidious and unconscious.

It happened to me some years ago. I was visiting Mexico from the US. And at the time, just as it is now, the political climate in the US was tense. And there were debates going on about immigration. And immigration was often synonymous with Mexicans. And Mexicans were all portrayed through a singular lens of negativity. There were stories about Mexicans being arrested at the border, stealing, fleecing the health care system, bringing disease.

I remember walking around on my first day in Guadalajara, a beautiful city. Watching people who were going to work and school. People who are laughing. People who were buying and selling in the market. At first I felt surprised, and then I was overwhelmed with shame. I realized that I had been so immersed in the American media's narrow coverage of Mexicans, that I had forgotten their humanity. And I could not have been more ashamed of myself.

In my language Igbo, the word for love—In Igbo, the word for love is Ifunanya. And it's literal translation is, "To see." So I would like to suggest today that this is a time for a new narrative. A narrative in which we truly see those about whom we speak.

Let us tell a different story. Let us tell the story differently. Let us remember that the movement of human beings on earth is not new. Human history is a story of movement and mingling. Let us remember that we are not just bones and flesh, we are emotional beings. We all share a desire to be valued, a desire to matter. Let us remember that dignity is as important as food.

When we speak of people who are in need, let us speak not only of their need, but also of what they love. What they resent, what wounds their pride, what they aspire to. What makes them laugh? Because if we do, then we are reminded of how similar we are in the midst of our differences. And we are better able to imagine ourselves in the same situation as those in need.

We cannot measure our humanity, but we can act on it. Our humanity is that glowing center in all of us. It is what makes us speak up about an injustice, even when that injustice does not personally affect us. It is what makes us aware that we are better off if our fellow human beings are better off. It is what made Emmanuel, in his cramped home full of relatives, still open his door to my parents and say, "We will make room for you."

I am not making the simplistic suggestion that all borders must be completely open. Because that is impractical. There might not be enough room for everyone. But there is certainly room to do more. There is room to honor more commitments. Room to bridge the divide between what has been promised, and what has been accomplished.

Emmanuel could've said, "No," to my parents. And he would've had understandable reasons for saying, "No." But he chose to say, "Yes." And his reason for saying yes was his humanity. We can create room for people. And today in this world that has been scarred by so much suffering, creating room for people is not only doable, it is a moral imperative. It is the moral imperative of our time.

And I would like to end with some words from the poet, Samuel Coleridge: "Work without hope draws nectar in a sieve, and hope without an object cannot live." Thank you.

Print Citations

CMS: Adichie, Chimamanda Ngozi. "Keynote Speech at World Humanitarian Day." Speech presented at World Humanitarian Day event, New York, NY, August, 2016. In *The Reference Shelf: Representative American Speeches 2015-2016*, edited by Betsy Maury, 173-75. Ipswich, MA: H.W. Wilson, 2016.

MLA: Adichie, Chimamanda Ngozi. "Keynote Speech at World Humanitarian Day." World Humanitarian Day event. New York, NY. August, 2016. Presentation. *The Reference Shelf: Representative American Speeches 2015-2016*. Ed. Betsy Maury. Ipswich: H.W. Wilson, 2016. 173-75. Print.

APA: Adichie, C.-N. (2016). Keynote speech at world humanitarian day. [Presentation]. *Speech presented at the World Humanitarian Day event*. New York, NY. In Betsy Maury (Ed.), *The reference shelf: Representative American speeches 2015-2016* (pp. 173-175). Ipswich, MA: H.W. Wilson. (Original work published 2016)

Opening Speech at the Rio Olympics

By Thomas Bach

In the opening speech to the 129th International Olympic Committee (IOC) Session in Rio de Janeiro, Brazil, President Thomas Bach of the IOC outlines some of the achievements of the Olympic committee and calls for unity among nations and athletes. A highlight of the speech and indeed a highlight of the Olympic Games, was the announcement of the first-ever Refugee Olympic Team. Bach says, "The refugee athletes will show the world that despite the unimaginable tragedies and suffering that they have faced, anyone can contribute to society through their talent, skills and most importantly, through the strength of the human spirit. The Refugee Olympic Team will represent the millions of refugees that have been left without a home because of conflict and war." Thomas Bach is a German lawyer and former Olympic fencer. He is the 9th and current President of the IOC.

Bem-vindo ao Rio de Janeiro! Welcome to the 129th IOC Session in beautiful Rio de Janeiro. It is exciting to be here, just a few days before the Opening Ceremony of the first-ever Olympic Games in South America. As the world's attention finally turns to the athletes and the competitions, all of us feel the anticipation building. The Cariocas are ready, the Brazilians are ready, the venues are ready and, most importantly, the athletes are ready.

After I arrived here, I went straight from the plane to the Olympic Village to check on the conditions for the athletes. I was happy to see that the initial challenges have been addressed in a positive spirit of cooperation with great support from the National Olympic Committees (NOCs) and our Brazilian hosts. It is a truly exceptional Olympic Village for all athletes. From the many conversations that I had with the athletes, I can tell you that they really appreciate the Olympic Village just as they appreciate the excellent competition and training venues. This athletes experience is the most important because the athletes are at the heart of the Olympic Games.

It has been a long and testing journey to get to this point: for all stakeholders of the Olympic Movement, for our Brazilian friends and for the IOC. It is no exaggeration to say that the Brazilians have been living through extraordinary times. The political and economic crisis in the country is unprecedented. It goes without saying that this situation has made the final preparations for the Olympic Games challenging.

Only if we remember what everyone had to overcome, we will be able to truly appreciate the unparalleled efforts of our Brazilian friends. It puts their efforts into

Delivered on August 1, 2016 in Rio de Janeiro, Brazil.

perspective and highlights their tremendous achievements. In a time when the country is divided politically, economically and socially, the transformation of Rio de Janeiro is truly historic. Rio de Janeiro would not be where it is today, without the Olympic Games as a catalyst. History will talk about a Rio de Janeiro before the Olympic Games and a much better Rio de Janeiro after the Olympic Games.

The extraordinary circumstances highlight the importance of teamwork. We would like to recognise the hard work of everyone in the Rio 2016 Organising Committee under the leadership of our dear colleague and friend, Carlos Nuzman. Thank you Carlos for your tireless perseverance. Our sincere thanks also go to Nawal El Moutawakel, the Chair of our Coordination Commission, and all her team for their great support and unwavering dedication.

Let me take this opportunity to thank all the Presidents and Secretary-Generals of the International Federations and of the National Olympic Committees. You have all demonstrated great solidarity. Thank you for your great contribution, understanding and flexibility under extraordinary circumstances. The Olympic family is always at its best whenever we are united in our resolve.

I would also like to highlight the crucial role of Mayor Eduardo Paes. His unwavering commitment and sheer boundless energy, made the difference. His vision was always that with the Olympic Games as a catalyst, you can transform the city. Today we can see that this vision is turning into reality. Thank you, Mr. Mayor, for your personal dedication and for being such a reliable partner.

We see the legacy of the Olympic Games is already transforming Rio de Janeiro. Just a few days ago, a study from a respected independent research foundation highlighted that thanks to the Olympic Games, Rio de Janeiro enjoyed greater and more equitable economic growth than any other city in Brazil. The study found that since Rio de Janeiro was chosen as host city, the per capita income in the city grew by over 30 percent. This study shows also that it was the poorest segment of the population that has benefited the most from this growth.

Rio de Janeiro is transforming in different ways. In just seven years, the number of people having access to good quality public transport has risen from just 18 percent in 2009 to 63 percent in 2016. The new metro line, the expanded bus routes and improved rail network will benefit Cariocas for generations to come. Olympic venues will be transformed into public parks and recreational areas for the local population after the Olympic Games. The handball venue will be turned into 4 public schools.

The Olympic Games transform the lives of people. During my visits to Rio de Janeiro, I was able to see first-hand how a number of education and social projects supported by the IOC and many of our Worldwide TOP Partners are making a difference in the lives of many young people. When I met these young girls and boys, I felt the confidence and motivation that sport gives them to succeed in life. Sport gives them the strength to shape their future and their communities. This is where we see the transformative power of sport in action.

This Olympic spirit of solidarity is also expressed in the creation of the first-ever Refugee Olympic Team. We will welcome the team tomorrow in our Session. They will compete alongside athletes from all other 206 National Olympic Committees. The refugee athletes will show the world that despite the unimaginable tragedies and suffering that they have faced, anyone can contribute to society through their talent, skills and most importantly, through the strength of the human spirit. The Refugee Olympic Team will represent the millions of refugees that have been left without a home because of conflict and war. The team will give hope to all refugees in the world. It will be a signal to the international community that refugees are our fellow human beings—that they are an enrichment to society just as they are an enrichment to our Olympic family.

In the weeks and days before coming to Rio de Janeiro, the IOC had to address the difficult situation regarding the recent allegations and revelations about doping in Russia. The findings in the McLaren report are very serious, in particular with regards to a system of doping allegedly orchestrated by the Russian Ministry of Sport. If proven true, such a contemptuous system of doping is an unprecedented attack on the integrity of sport and on the Olympic Games. Just after the report findings were made public a couple of days ago, the IOC addressed this matter immediately. With the Olympic Games just a few days away, we had to take action even though the McLaren report is not yet finished and the Russian side has not been heard yet. The decision of the IOC Executive Board was unanimous and it followed the principles of the Olympic Summit, which were also unanimously agreed by all stakeholders.

We took immediate measures to shed full light on the allegations and more actions and sanctions will follow if necessary. With regard to the participation of Russian athletes at these Olympic Games, we had to take the necessary decisions. Because of the seriousness of the allegations we could not uphold the presumption of innocence for Russian athletes. On the other hand, we cannot deprive an athlete of the human right to be given the opportunity to prove his or her innocence. You cannot punish a human being for the failures of his or her government if he or she is not implicated. These principles are now being implemented. This decision is about justice. Justice has to be independent from politics.

Whoever responds to a violation of the law with another violation of the law is destroying justice. We have a busy agenda ahead of us at this IOC Session. As always, we should use this IOC Session to look further ahead to the future trends that will shape the role of sport in society.

If we want to make a difference in the world today, we must engage with youth. Young people including many athletes are living in a new digital reality. Young people are digitally "always on". This new world has huge implications for the future of the Olympic Movement.

With the many options that youth have today we cannot expect them to naturally come to sport. We have to go where they are. Because these questions are so fundamentally important, we visited the heart of the digital world in Silicon Valley earlier this year. There we asked the leaders of the digital world the following questions: Will there still be sport in 20 years from now? Is sport in competition with the digital world for the time of the youth? Can the digital world inspire young people to practise sport?

I am happy to report that all these digital leaders reassured us that there will still be sport in 20 years from now. They also wanted to make us believe that we are not in competition for the time of the youth. They told us that by embracing the possibilities of the digital world, the role of sport can even be enhanced. By making better use of digital channels, we can reach an even greater number of young people.

The challenge for us is to ensure that people do not just move their fingers to move a mouse, or move their lips to give commands to a computer, or move their eyes only to watch a screen. Our task is to inspire people to practise sport, to move and engage in physical activity.

At these Olympic Games, there will be more digital content than ever before. In fact, we expect double the amount of content on digital platforms than on television. These Olympic Games will be truly digital. You will see that we are already applying the lessons from the visit to Silicon Valley. New technologies like Virtual Reality, 360-degree cameras and many other cutting-edge digital advances allow us to tell the story of the Olympic Games like it has never been told before.

We are bringing the digital world right to the athletes. They will be among the first to benefit from our visit to Silicon Valley. Among the many opportunities, they will have the chance to engage with Gerald Andal, the first digital Artist in Residence at the Olympic Village. He will produce video art on Vine. For all of you who are not familiar with Vine, like I was until a few months ago: this is a social media platform that allows you to share six and a half seconds of video clips. I have to admit that I was a bit sceptical when I first heard of it. But I was converted in about six and a half seconds after I saw the fantastic images and emotions that can be expressed. It completely captures the magic of the digital world.

Young people are living in this digital world and this is where we need to go. This is why I am excited to tell you that only a year and a half since we approved this project with Olympic Agenda 2020: we are launching the Olympic Channel. With the Closing Ceremony we will bring the Olympic Movement into the digital world. This will be another milestone for us and the beginning of a new journey. We will enter a new world.

With the Olympic Channel, the inspirational power of the Olympic Games will no longer be limited to seventeen days every four years. With this Olympic Agenda 2020 project, we will spread Olympic Values in between and beyond the Olympic Games. This digital platform will be available anytime, anywhere, on any device. Sport fans and all people around the world will have continuous exposure to Olympic sports and athletes, 24 hours a day, 365 days a year.

This represents a unique opportunity for everyone. This is demonstrated by the great interest and support we are getting from so many of our partners—from athletes, International Federations, National Olympic Committees, Rights-Holding Broadcasters, Worldwide TOP Partners, as well as from major social media platforms.

The Olympic Channel will continue to evolve, as the digital world evolves.

We are at an important juncture when we can shape our future. As our founder Pierre de Coubertin explained, Olympism is a pilgrimage to the past and an act of faith in the future.

Now is the time for faith in the future. A new world of opportunities is opening up for us. Let us be united in this faith and shape the future together.

In this spirit, I now declare the 129th Session of the International Olympic Committee open.

Print Citations

CMS: Bach, Thomas. "Opening Speech at the Rio Olympics." Rio de Janeiro, Brazil, August, 2016. In *The Reference Shelf: Representative American Speeches 2015-2016*, edited by Betsy Maury, 176-80. Ipswich, MA: H.W. Wilson, 2016.

MLA: Bach, Thomas. "Opening Speech at the Rio Olympics." Rio de Janeiro, Brazil. August, 2016. Presentation. *The Reference Shelf: Representative American Speeches 2015-2016*. Ed. Betsy Maury. Ipswich: H.W. Wilson, 2016. 176-80. Print.

APA: Bach, T. (2016). Opening speech at the Rio olympics. [Presentation]. Rio de Janeiro, Brazil. In Betsy Maury (Ed.), *The reference shelf: Representative American speeches 2015-2016* (pp. 176-180). Ipswich, MA: H.W. Wilson. (Original work published 2016)

Speech After "Brexit" Vote

By David Cameron

In this speech, Prime Minister of the United Kingdom, David Cameron informs the British public that he will step down from his post after the country voted to leave the European Union. The "Brexit" vote, as it came to be called shocked both Britons and Europeans. In June of 2016, the United Kingdom voted on a referendum to continue membership of the EU, which Cameron had promised to hold. Though Cameron supported continued membership, the Leave campaign was successful in winning exit from the European Union. David Cameron is a British politician who was the prime minister of the United Kingdom from May 2010 to July 2016. He served as the leader of the Conservative Party from December 2005 to July 2016.

The country has just taken part in a giant democratic exercise—perhaps the biggest in our history. Over 33 million people—from England, Scotland, Wales, Northern Ireland and Gibraltar—have all had their say.

We should be proud of the fact that in these islands we trust the people with these big decisions.

We not only have a parliamentary democracy, but on questions about the arrangements for how we are governed, there are times when it is right to ask the people themselves, and that is what we have done.

The British people have voted to leave the European Union, and their will must be respected.

I want to thank everyone who took part in the campaign on my side of the argument, including all those who put aside party differences to speak in what they believed was the national interest.

And let me congratulate all those who took part in the "Leave" campaign—for the spirited and passionate case that they made.

The will of the British people is an instruction that must be delivered. It was not a decision that was taken lightly, not least because so many things were said by so many different organizations about the significance of this decision.

So there can be no doubt about the result.

Delivered on June 24, 2016 in London, England..

Across the world people have been watching the choice that Britain has made. I would reassure those markets and investors that Britain's economy is fundamentally strong.

And I would also reassure Brits living in European countries, and European citizens living here, that there will be no immediate changes in your circumstances. There will be no initial change in the way our people can travel, in the way our goods can move or the way our services can be sold.

We must now prepare for a negotiation with the European Union. This will need to involve the full engagement of the Scottish, Welsh and Northern Ireland governments to ensure that the interests of all parts of our United Kingdom are protected and advanced.

But above all this will require strong, determined and committed leadership.

I am very proud and very honored to have been prime minister of this country for six years.

I believe we have made great steps, with more people in work than ever before in our history, with reforms to welfare and education, increasing people's life chances, building a bigger and stronger society, keeping our promises to the poorest people in the world, and enabling those who love each other to get married whatever their sexuality.

But above all restoring Britain's economic strength, and I am grateful to everyone who has helped to make that happen.

I have also always believed that we have to confront big decisions—not duck them.

That's why we delivered the first coalition government in 70 years to bring our economy back from the brink. It's why we delivered a fair, legal and decisive referendum in Scotland. And why I made the pledge to renegotiate Britain's position in the European Union and hold a referendum on our membership, and have carried those things out.

I fought this campaign in the only way I know how—which is to say directly and passionately what I think and feel—head, heart and soul.

I held nothing back.

I was absolutely clear about my belief that Britain is stronger, safer and better off inside the European Union, and I made clear the referendum was about this and this alone—not the future of any single politician, including myself.

But the British people have made a very clear decision to take a different path, and as such I think the country requires fresh leadership to take it in this direction.

I will do everything I can as prime minister to steady the ship over the coming weeks and months, but I do not think it would be right for me to try to be the captain that steers our country to its next destination.

This is not a decision I have taken lightly, but I do believe it is in the national interest to have a period of stability and then the new leadership required.

There is no need for a precise timetable today, but in my view we should aim to have a new prime minister in place by the start of the Conservative Party conference in October.

Delivering stability will be important, and I will continue in the post as prime minister with my cabinet for the next three months. The cabinet will meet on Monday.

The governor of the Bank of England is making a statement about the steps that the bank and the Treasury are taking to reassure financial markets. We will also continue taking forward the important legislation that we set before Parliament in the Queen's Speech. And I have spoken to Her Majesty, the Queen, this morning to advise her of the steps that I am taking.

A negotiation with the European Union will need to begin under a new prime minister, and I think it is right that this new prime minister takes the decision about when to trigger Article 50 and start the formal and legal process of leaving the EU.

I will attend the European Council next week to explain the decision the British people have taken and my own decision.

The British people have made a choice. That not only needs to be respected—but those on the losing side of the argument, myself included, should help to make it work.

Britain is a special country.

We have so many great advantages.

A parliamentary democracy where we resolve great issues about our future through peaceful debate.

A great trading nation, with our science and arts, our engineering and our creativity respected the world over.

And while we are not perfect, I do believe we can be a model of a multiracial, multifaith democracy, where people can come and make a contribution and rise to the very highest that their talent allows.

Although leaving Europe was not the path I recommended, I am the first to praise our incredible strengths.

I have said before that Britain can survive outside the European Union, and indeed that we could find a way.

Now the decision has been made to leave, we need to find the best way.

And I will do everything I can to help.

I love this country—and I feel honored to have served it.

And I will do everything I can in the future to help this great country succeed.

Print Citations

CMS: Cameron, David. "Speech After 'Brexit' Vote." London, England, June, 2016. In *The Reference Shelf: Representative American Speeches 2015-2016*, edited by Betsy Maury, 181-83. Ipswich, MA: H.W. Wilson, 2016.

MLA: Cameron, David. "Speech After 'Brexit' Vote." London, England. June, 2016. Presentation. *The Reference Shelf: Representative American Speeches 2015-2016*. Ed. Betsy Maury. Ipswich: H.W. Wilson, 2016. 181-83. Print.

APA: Cameron, D. (2016). Speech after the "Brexit" vote. [Presentation]. London, England. In Betsy Maury (Ed.), *The reference shelf: Representative American speeches 2015-2016* (pp. 181-183). Ipswich, MA: H.W. Wilson. (Original work published 2016)

Index